RICHARD V. PIERARD received his B.A. and M.A. degrees from California State College at Los Angeles and his Ph.D. in history from the University of Iowa. He was a Fulbright Scholar at the University of Hamburg, Germany, and is currently Associate Professor of History at Indiana State University. He is a member of the Baptist General Conference.

The Unequal Yoke

Evangelical Perspectives

John Warwick Montgomery, General Editor

How Black Is the Gospel?
by Tom Skinner
The Unequal Yoke
by Richard V. Pierard

RICHARD V. PIERARD

The Unequal Yoke

Evangelical Christianity
and Political Conservatism

J. B. Lippincott Company
Philadelphia and New York

Foreword

A Perspective on "Evangelical Perspectives"

Across the centuries the Christian church has faced two perennial challenges: the maintenance of a pure testimony, and the application of revealed truth to the total life of man. Though these two tasks interlock (since application of the truth is impossible if the truth is lost, and truth without application stands self-condemned), theology has generally devoted itself now to the one, now to the other, and the cause of Christ has suffered from the imbalance. "These ought ye to have done, and not to leave the other undone" stands as a perpetual judgment over the church's history.

Today's theology and church life display such deleterious polarization in an especially gross manner. At the liberal end of the theological spectrum, efforts to become "relevant" have succeeded so well that the church has become indistinguishable from the ideological and societal evils she is supposed to combat. Among the fundamentalists, in contrast, God's revealed truth often serves as a wall to block the church off from the live issues and compelling challenges of a world in crisis. Relevance

5

without truth, or truth without relevance: these dual
schizophrenias go far in explaining why contemporary
man finds it easy to ignore the Christian message.

Evangelical Perspectives is a series of books designed
specifically to overcome these false dichotomies. Historic
Christian theology—the Christianity of the Apostles'
Creed, of the Protestant Reformation, and of the eighteenth-century Evangelical Revival—is taken with full se-
riousness, and is shown to be entirely compatible with
the best of contemporary scholarship. Contributors to
this series are united in rejecting the defensive posture
which has so often created the impression that new
knowledge poses a genuine threat to the Christian gospel. Axiomatic to the present series is the conviction that
new discoveries serve but to confirm and deepen the
faith once delivered to the saints.

At the same time, those participating in this project
find little comfort in the reiteration of ancient truth for
its own sake. Our age faces staggering challenges which
can hardly be met by the repetition of formulas—certainly not by the negativistic codes of a fundamentalism
which tilts against windmills that have long since fallen
into decay. The race problem, social revolution, political
change, new sexual freedom, the revival of the occult,
the advent of the space age: these are areas of modern
life that demand fresh analysis on the basis of the eternal
verities set forth in the Word of One who is the same
yesterday, today, and forever.

Out of the flux of the current theological situation
nothing but flux appears to be emerging. What is
needed is a firm foundation on which to build an all-
embracing and genuinely relevant theological perspective for the emerging twenty-first century. The authors
of the present volumes are endeavoring to offer just such

a perspective—an *evangelical* perspective, a perspective arising from the biblical evangel—as the one path through the maze of contemporary life.

It is the hope of the editor that upon the solid Reformation base of a fully authoritative Scripture, the present series will offer its readers the Renaissance ideal of the Christian as *uomo universale.* Such an orientation could revolutionize theology in our time, and ground a new age of commitment and discovery comparable to that of the sixteenth century. As in that day, new worlds are opening up, and just as a religious viewpoint reflecting the dying medieval age was unable to meet the challenge then, so today's secular theologies are incapable of pointing the way now. The Christ of the Bible, through whom all without exception have been created and redeemed: he alone is Way, Truth, Life—and Perspective!

JOHN W. MONTGOMERY
General Editor

Preface

This book is the outgrowth of a deep concern on my part about the health of evangelical Christianity. I have been grieved by the repeated accusations of liberals that we are the handmaidens of the Far Right and embarrassed by the pronouncements of leading figures in our ranks that seem to give substance to these charges. A great many evangelicals, especially among the younger generation, feel as I do, and several of us have articulated our concerns in the book *Protest and Politics: Christianity and Contemporary Affairs.*[1] The enthusiastic critical response to the book and its healthy sales level indicate how widespread the opinion is that evangelical Christianity is too closely linked to political conservatism.

I am fully aware of the pitfalls in trying to make generalizations about such a large and diverse grouping as evangelical Christianity. Thus, I have selected examples to reinforce my contentions from those speakers and au-

[1] Greenwood, S.C.: Attic Press, 1968.

thors who are connected with denominations, organizations, schools, and publications that are generally regarded as evangelical in their orientation or who personally identify themselves as such.

This examination of the problem which I feel is crippling orthodox Christianity is not meant to be vindictive or hypercritical, but rather it is aimed at bringing the matter out in the open so that corrective measures may be initiated. Moreover, it is not intended to be an exhaustive study but rather the identification of some trends in evangelical thought and action. I am cognizant that many exceptions exist to these and that some of the people have changed their views since the time they were expressed, and I am encouraged whenever this is the case. It is my sincere conviction that, if the trend toward political, economic, and social conservatism is not reversed, evangelical Christianity will soon be facing a crisis of disastrous proportions. In fact, its very survival in the 1970's may well depend on whether it can escape from the Unequal Yoke. If nothing is done, evangelicalism in the 1980's will be relegated to the status of a small and insignificant sect. God forbid that this should happen!

There are many people whose encouragement and assistance at various stages of my work deserve to be recognized. They include Robert G. Clouse, Rudolph W. Heinze, Orley R. Herron, James E. Johnson, Robert D. Linder, Ross T. Lucas, John Warwick Montgomery, Donald E. Pitzer, Herbert J. Rissler, Donald B. Scheick, W. Richard Stephens, and Ellis K. Yaw. The Inter-Library Loan Service of the Cunningham Memorial Library at Indiana State University was invaluable in helping to secure material. I also would like to thank the libraries at Christian Theological Seminary, Southern

Baptist Theological Seminary, Moody Bible Institute, Concordia Teachers College, and Trinity Evangelical Divinity School for their kind cooperation and assistance. But above all these is my debt of gratitude to my wife, Charlene, for her great help and encouragement in preparing the book and typing the manuscript.

R. V. P.
Department of History
Indiana State University

Contents

I To What Is the Evangelical Church Yoked?

Be ye not unequally yoked together with unbelievers: for what fellowship hath righteousness with unrighteousness? and what communion hath light with darkness? And what concord hath Christ with Belial? or what part hath he that believeth with an infidel? . . . Wherefore come out from among them, and be ye separate, saith the Lord. (II Corinthians 6:14–15, 17 KJV)

Take my yoke upon you, and learn from me; for I am gentle and lowly in heart, and you will find rest for your souls. For my yoke is easy, and my burden is light. (Matthew 11:29–30)

There's good reason to mix religion and politics. . . . We have found that fundamentalist Christians and conservative politicians have a lot in common. (The Rev. Dr. Charles Bishop, Baptist minister and chaplain of the Georgia Senate) [1]

The N.A.E.'s outlook on political and economic affairs is so deeply committed to nationalistic, laissez-faire ultra-

[1] Quoted in Robert G. Sherrill, "Bob Jones University: New Curricula for Bigotry," *Nation*, Vol. CC (March 29, 1965), p. 333.

conservatism that it shocks even the most chastened Liberal Protestant. (William G. McLoughlin) [2]

The Church Stands Accused

Conservative Christians are often accused of linking their faith to right-wing politics, a contention which is made both in conservative and liberal circles. The outspoken black evangelical William E. Pannell charged that conservative Christianity perpetuates the myth of white supremacy and associates the faith with American patriotism, free enterprise, and the Republican Party.[3] Methodist Harold Kuhn wrote in *Christianity Today* that "there are those who, while professing full loyalty to the teachings of their Lord, assume a stance that not only smacks of social irresponsibility but also at times allies itself with the forces having vested interest in maintaining social injustice." [4] Bob Thieme, pastor of the large fundamentalist Berachah Church in Houston, said that nine times out of ten, people who are conservative about the Scriptures will be conservative politically.[5] The liberally oriented *Christian Century* has repeatedly chided those to the right of its theological position for their social and political conservatism, and in a particularly hard-hitting editorial in 1965 jumped the "new"

[2] William G. McLoughlin, "Is There a Third Force in Christendom?" *Daedalus*, Vol. XCVI (Winter, 1967), pp. 60–61.

[3] William E. Pannell, *My Friend, the Enemy* (Waco, Texas: Word, 1968), p. 53.

[4] Harold B. Kuhn, "Evangelicals and the Prophetic Message," *Christianity Today*, Vol. IX (May 7, 1965), p. 55.

[5] Quoted in Willie Morris, "Houston's Superpatriots," *Harper's*, Vol. CCXXIII (October, 1961), p. 54.

evangelicals for being on the wrong side of the burning social questions of the day.[6]

Does a close relationship between conservative theology and conservative sociopolitical views actually exist? Unfortunately, it does, and many evangelical spokesmen are quite satisfied with it, as evidenced by their actions and public statements. Take voting behavior, for example. A Purdue University sociologist, Jeffrey K. Hadden, made a survey of seven hundred American Baptist Convention clergymen in which he asked them to identify their theological position and how they voted in the 1964 Presidential election. The results were most revealing: [7]

Theological Position	Number	*Percentage Who Voted for* Goldwater
Fundamentalist	49	69
Conservative	383	51
Neo-orthodox	128	11
Liberal	140	5

Given these data, it is not difficult to understand why fundamentalists like evangelist Billy James Hargis declared that the election of Barry Goldwater together with a conservative Congress "would be the millennium" or why Lawrence Lautenbach, dean of the College of Business at Bob Jones University, said his election would be a "step in the right direction." [8]

[6] "Demythologizing Neoevangelicalism," *Christian Century,* Vol. LXXXII (September 15, 1965), pp. 1115–16.

[7] Quoted in McLoughlin, *Daedalus,* p. 67. For the entire results of the "Hadden Survey" see *Transaction,* July–August, 1967.

[8] *The New York Times,* August 9, 1964, p. 55.

The reader should not dismiss these as merely expressions of ultraconservatism and hence of little or no significance. *Christianity Today,* the principal voice of evangelical Christianity and a journal noted for its moderation and scholarly bearing, recently editorialized:

> The eager ecclesiastical advocates of a single left-wing politico-socio-economic line must not be allowed, through the default of a silent laity, exclusive claim to the Church's prestige to promote their social doctrines. Often their views must be opposed as decidedly anti-Christian.[9]

To illustrate further, a well-known evangelical historian and prominent churchman in the Southern Presbyterian denomination published a study of American history which endeavors to prove that democracy and Christianity are incompatible and maintains in no uncertain terms that government action to promote the social welfare of its citizens is based on anti-Christian premises.[10]

The ties linking evangelical Christianity to political conservatism are so numerous and pervasive that it is possible to say the two are "yoked together." But is this a desirable situation? Is the evangelical church trading on dangerous ground? The answer which comes from Holy Scripture is clear and unequivocal: "Be ye not unequally yoked together" (II Corinthians 6:14). What this means is that the Christian should avoid close ties that would link him with unbelievers in pagan ways of thought and action. A fundamental opposition exists between the way of Christ and the way of the world. A

[9] "Who Speaks for the Church?" *Christianity Today,* Vol. XI (June 9, 1967), p. 27.

[10] C. Gregg Singer, *A Theological Interpretation of American History* (Nutley, N.J.: The Craig Press, 1964).

church that is conformed to the world (Romans 12:2) will never provide leadership there. Its values will be dictated either by Christ and the Word of God or the secular "success culture" in which it finds itself. As will be shown below, the evangelical church has tied itself to the *status quo* of contemporary middle-class America and traded its prophetic ministry for a pottage of public acclaim and economic well-being.

The yoke of Christ is easy and his burden is light, whereas the yoke of political conservatism is like that of the ungodly King Rehoboam (I Kings 12:14). The vital question facing conservative Christianity in the 1970's is whether it will exchange the worldly yoke for that of Christ. In short, will the church come out and separate itself from those who are manipulating it for their own selfish interests and fulfill the prophetic task which the Head of the church has intended for it?

Evangelical Christianity

Before proceeding further, it would be advisable to define the two terms which will appear throughout this study: "evangelical Christianity" and "political conserv- atism." The first of these will be used interchangeably with such expressions as "evangelicalism," "conservative theology," and "orthodox Christianity." The minimal definition is perhaps that of Edward John Carnell: "Or- thodoxy is that branch of Christendom which limits the ground of religious authority to the Bible. No other rule of faith and practice is acknowledged." [11] Thus, those who deny that the Bible is the sole source of religious

[11] Edward John Carnell, *The Case for Orthodox Theology* (Phila- delphia: Westminster, 1959), p. 13.

authority would be excluded. Most definitions, however, are more detailed.

Harold Ockenga feels an evangelical is one who holds or conforms to what the majority of Protestants regard as the fundamental doctrines of the Gospel, such as the Trinity, the fallen condition of man, Christ's atonement for sin, salvation by faith alone without good works, and regeneration by the Holy Spirit. The evangelical's doctrinal position is that of "orthodox or creedal Christianity." Thus, he holds to the "objective truths" stated in the New Testament and the great creeds and confessions of Christendom such as the Chalcedonian and the later Reformed confessions such as those of Augsburg, Heidelberg, and Westminster. Finally, he depends on the Bible as the authoritative Word of God and the norm of judgment in faith and practice.[12]

An organization which seeks to bring about cooperation among evangelical Christians, the National Association of Evangelicals (N.A.E.), adopted a seven-point doctrinal statement to which its member churches are expected to subscribe. Beliefs listed here include (1) the inspiration, infallibility, and authority of the Bible, (2) the Trinity, (3) the deity of Christ, together with his Virgin Birth, sinless life, miracles, vicarious and atoning death through his shed blood, bodily resurrection, ascension to the right hand of the Father, and personal return in power and glory, (4) regeneration by the Holy Spirit necessary for the salvation of lost and sinful man, (5) the present ministry of the Holy Spirit enabling the Christian to lead a godly life, (6) the resurrection of the saved and lost, the one to eternal life and the other to eternal damnation, and (7) the spiritual unity of believ-

[12] Harold John Ockenga, "Resurgent Evangelical Leadership," *Christianity Today*, Vol. V (October 10, 1960), pp. 11–12.

ers in Jesus Christ.[13] Some evangelical agencies such as foreign mission societies and Christian schools often have even more detailed creedal statements than this.

It seems, then, that the evangelical is identified by his emphasis upon the inspiration and authority of the Scriptures and the need for individual spiritual regeneration (salvation) through faith in Jesus Christ and the action of the Holy Spirit. The death of Christ for the sins of mankind makes possible the restoration of fellowship and communion between the Creator and humanity. In conservative theology there is a continuum of doctrinal solidarity on these basics reaching from fundamentalism to many who would prefer to identify themselves as "evangelicals" or "confessionalists." [14] The confessing evangelical differs from the fundamentalist particularly in that he is seriously trying to place conservative Christianity in the mainstream of contemporary life and make the orthodox position a live option for modern man. Because of their intense emphasis upon the preservation of their heritage, fundamentalists tend to be especially critical of the neoevangelicals (a term allegedly coined by Ockenga) whom they see in a posture of potential or actual compromise. This should, however, not be allowed to obscure the fact that both groups belong very much to the same Christian family and therefore have a common interest in the proclamation of the Gospel of Jesus Christ.

[13] James DeForest Murch, *Co-operation Without Compromise* (Grand Rapids, Mich.: Eerdmans, 1956), pp. 65–66.

[14] On the precise meaning of—and distinction between—these terms in contemporary conservative theology, see the contributions by Carl F. H. Henry ("evangelical") and John Warwick Montgomery ("confessionalist") in Robert Campbell, O.P. (ed.), *Spectrum of Protestant Beliefs* (Milwaukee: Bruce Publishing Company, 1968).

Political Conservatism

How may political conservatism be defined? This is
somewhat more difficult to do because there is such a
wide diversity of views among conservatives in the
United States, and probably no two people would agree
completely on a listing of conservative tenets. Generally
speaking, however, most conservatives would go along
with the following ideas, which are expressed in such
places as the *National Review* and Senator Barry Goldwater's widely received book *The Conscience of a Conservative.*[15] Some adherents to the position will of course
reject or modify some of the points while others may feel
the list does not go far enough, but keeping these reserva-
tions in mind one can say that this is a fair description of
current conservative beliefs.

First, individual freedom is a primary concern of conservatism, that is, achieving as much freedom as possible
but at the same time maintaining the social order. Freedom can only exist in a state of order, but that political
power which might threaten freedom must be kept
within bounds. The power of the government must be
limited to its legitimate functions of maintaining internal order, administering justice, and providing protection from foreign enemies. Since government has the
tendency to expand its power indefinitely, the American
founding fathers drew up the Constitution which limited the federal government to specific (delegated)
powers, reserved all other powers to the states and the
people, and divided the government's power among
three separate branches, the executive, legislative, and
judicial. The framers of the Constitution rejected de-

[15] New York: Macfadden Books, 1960.

mocracy (the tyranny of the masses) by creating a republic which both was restricted in its scope of authority
and dispersed public authority among several levels of
government so as to forestall the central government
from gathering all power into its hands. "States' rights"
in particular is the bulwark against encroachment by
"big government."

Unfortunately, the twentieth century has witnessed—
alleges the conservative—a frightening expansion of federal power which is clearly in violation of the Constitution. In such areas as civil rights, social-welfare programs,
education, electric power, agriculture, urban renewal,
public housing, and highway construction the federal
government has been "usurping" the powers of the
states. The conservative fears this as the accumulation of
power in a central government remote from the people
and a patent violation of the principle that local problems can best be taken care of by those who are most
directly concerned with them. Thus, federal spending
should be cut back as rapidly as possible, and the government should curtail its activities, especially in the social
and economic field.

The right of each person to property and to enjoy the
fruits of his labor is a basic theme among conservatives.
Freedom and property are inseparable, and so government encroachment on property rights must be halted.
The government may rightfully claim only the tax
money needed to carry out its delegated powers and
nothing more. Further, the progressive (graduated) income tax is unjust because it violates property rights by
confiscating the wealth of the more industrious persons
and redistributing it to the less productive. All necessary
restrictions on economic individualism (free enterprise)
should be lifted, and the government should be discour-

aged from engaging in economic endeavors that compete
with privately owned ventures. Also, more conservatives
look askance at the power of large labor organizations.
The unseen hand of the free market should be allowed
to regulate business activities and thus will elevate the
general economic level of American society. Unwarranted government interference in the economy violates
the property rights of the individual producers and will
result in untold mischief.

The conservative is fearful of "socialism" or "collectivism" and sees the welfare state as a significant step in
that direction. It places the individual at the mercy of
the state, because the enormous amount of taxes needed
to support welfare programs divests him of the means to
provide for his personal needs, and the state assumes the
responsibility of providing for those requirements. Dependence on the government will inexorably lead to
bondage to the absolute state, since welfarism destroys
the individual's sense of initiative and self-reliance. If
the personal responsibility to care for one's needs is
taken from a man, he has lost the will and opportunity
to be free.

It is clear that the conservative is convinced of the
moral superiority of America, although he believes that
many of the traditional values and structures are eroding.
He loves his country and expresses his patriotism and
loyalty in various ways, such as voting in elections, running for public office, displaying the flag, and maintaining membership in civic and patriotic organizations. He
looks with pride upon American achievements in the
past, including military ones, and has little patience with
left-wing critics of the American system or those who
emphasize the more unpleasant aspects of American history. This person vigorously opposes any attempts to
compromise American sovereignty through world-gov-

ernment schemes and because of this tends to look upon the United Nations with some suspicion. Also, conservatives usually manifest a certain measure of religious commitment—though the nature and quality of it vary widely among individuals. Frequently this religious faith is identified in some way with "Americanism."

A primary concern is the menace of communism. Conservatives are fearful that the United States is threatened by this alien doctrine and that not enough has been done to counter the threat. Instead of seeking victory over communism, the American government has adopted a defensive posture by falling back on such dubious policies as military alliances, foreign economic aid, cultural-exchange programs, and disarmament negotiations with communist regimes. Peace is the proper goal of American policy, but it must be one in which freedom and justice will prevail. Nuclear war with the Soviet Union, as frightful as that might appear, would be preferable to submission to communist tyranny. Patriotic Americans should be informed about the true nature of communism and must strive to counter left-wing thinking that weakens this country's ability to resist communist subversion. This can be achieved by educating the younger generation in the values of American constitutional government and the free-enterprise system and urging the national leaders to uphold these values and to maintain a military establishment superior to that of the communist foe.

Origins of the Unequal Yoke

At this point the inevitable question arises: how did evangelical Christianity become so closely linked to twentieth-century political conservatism? This is not

easy to answer and considerable research needs to be
done to ferret out the origins of the marriage of orthodox
theology to the social, economic, and political *status
quo*. This writer is prepared to suggest some possible
explanations but the reader must be cautioned that these
are no more than tentative. It is hoped that evangelical
scholars in increasing numbers will direct their attention
to exploring the problem and provide more precise answers than are now available.

If the church seems tame and subdued today, it was
not always that way. Biblical religion traditionally manifested a distinct social dimension. Moses was the leader
of an oppressed people whom he led out of bondage into
a normal place in the human community. The Old Testament law had the intent of throwing the "arms of
protection around the less favored members of society"
and was a bulwark against the slave economy which
cursed the other contemporary societies of antiquity.
Amos was the prototype of the protesting minority when
he called for justice to roll down like waters and righteousness like an everlasting stream, and he applied the
divine plumb line to such social abuses as race, poverty,
war, real-estate profiteering, and discrimination against
minorities. Most of the Hebrew prophets made a "surgi-
cal analysis" of prevailing social conditions and pro-
nounced God's verdict of judgment.[16]

In the New Testament a full-blown social ethic
emerged which was revolutionary in its implications and
oriented toward meeting human needs. As Sherwood
Wirt puts it: "A generous, friendly humanitarian interest in people breathes from every page from Matthew to

[16] Sherwood Eliot Wirt, *The Social Conscience of the Evangelical*
(New York: Harper & Row, 1968), pp. 8–11.

Revelation." [17] Jesus consorted with sinners and chose as
disciples peasants instead of influential citizens. When
he took a whip to the money changers in the temple,
journeyed through instead of around Samaria, plucked
grain on the Sabbath, and ate without ceremonially
washing his hands, he demonstrated how human values
were more important than maintenance of the *status
quo*. What he did to the pigs of Gadara revealed a
shocking disrespect for private property. Jesus taught
that the best way to show the love of God is to love one's
fellowmen. He elevated human life by saying "of how
much more value is a man than a sheep" (Matthew
12:12). He fed the hungry, healed the sick, enabled the
crippled to walk, and gave sight to the blind—to mention only a few of his selfless acts to raise the level of
human life. The standard by which the nations were to
be judged was social action: had they fed the hungry,
given drink to the thirsty, welcomed the stranger,
clothed the naked, cared for the sick, and visited the
prisoners (Matthew 25:31–46)? Finally, he identified
with the totality of humanity by taking upon himself the
burden of sin of all mankind, thereby opening the way of
reconciliation to God. [18]

The church was founded to spread the Gospel
throughout the world and to communicate the human
concern of the Son of God. One of the earliest actions of
the church at Jerusalem was to make formal provision
for caring for the physical needs of widows. The Mace-
donian churches sent financial assistance to the impover-
ished in Palestine. Pure religion was defined as minister-

[17] *Ibid.*, p. 12.
[18] David O. Moberg, *Inasmuch: Christian Social Responsibility in
20th Century America* (Grand Rapids, Mich.: Eerdmans, 1965), chap.
2.

ing to orphans and widows, and the faith of a person who did nothing to care for the bodily needs of his brethren was labeled as dead (James 1:27, 2:15–17). In subsequent centuries Christians were in the forefront of meeting human needs by founding hospitals, orphanages, and schools, and intervening to moderate the harshness of political and social structures. Billy Graham correctly recognized this when he said that "as a result of the coming of Christ Jesus, thousands of Christians through the ages have given their lives to help their neighbor, to relieve poverty, to care for the sick." [19]

The nineteenth century saw a blossoming of Christian social concern under the influence of Wesley and the evangelical revival movements. Christians regarded individual regeneration as not only the climax of evangelistic endeavor but also a chief means of social reform. They saw a direct relation between personal salvation and community improvement. Conversion had the effect of shifting the individual's controlling motivation from self-interest to Christian concern, and this marked not the end but only the beginning of life. The Gospel demanded a dedication of one's life to the service of God and fellowman. Society would be reconstructed through the power of the Gospel, and evils like slavery, poverty, and greed would be eliminated. The soul-winning impulse moved Christians to systematic effort to relieve the miseries of the urban poor by the distribution of food and clothing, aiding immigrants in finding employment, and providing medical aid for the lowest classes. As Christians brought about changes in the social, political, and moral condition of the world, the way would be

[19] Graham, *Social Injustice* (Minneapolis, BGEA, 1967), p. 4. (An *Hour of Decision* radio sermon.)

opened to a millennial reign of justice and righteousness.[20]

However, new forces were at work in the post-Civil War years that contributed to the gradual erosion of this fervent social concern and the transformation of evangelical Christianity into a bastion of the *status quo*. For one thing, the enormity of the problems of industrialization and urbanization simply overwhelmed the capabilities of this small-scale religious philanthropy. Urban problems like substandard housing, poverty, unemployment, disease, and crime were too much for the churches with their limited resources to cope with effectively. Many of the faithful shook their heads in despair and concluded there was little they could do about the wretched social conditions except pray and try to evangelize their neighbors. Added to this was the retreat from the inner cities by established Protestant congregations, leaving many slum areas virtually devoid of churches.

A second factor was that orthodox preachers were engaged in fighting a defensive war against the new ideas that menaced the foundations of Christianity. Darwinism, higher criticism, and Marxism, to mention a few, penetrated the ranks of the faithful, and evangelical leaders devoted much of their energy to negative refutation. Necessary as such activity doubtless was, it nonetheless sapped the church of considerable vitality and diverted its attention from crying social needs.

One of the most serious difficulties which beset the church was the reaction to the social gospel. Many Christians came to see that the only way to cope with the

[20] Timothy L. Smith, *Revivalism and Social Reform: American Protestantism on the Eve of the Civil War* (Nashville, Tenn.: Abingdon, 1957), chap. 10; Bruce L. Shelley, *Evangelicalism in America* (Grand Rapids, Mich.: Eerdmans, 1967), pp. 51–52.

massive problems of society was to involve the state in
social reform, and this meant striking at economic privilege and modifying the social order. The social gospelers
were directly in the pre-1860 evangelical tradition, but
their movement came increasingly to manifest secular
tendencies, while the leaders' interest in biblical Christianity rapidly declined. As the social gospel advocates
moved in the direction of theological liberalism, animosities between them and the orthodox became increasingly bitter. Contributing to this growing hostility was
the vigorous rejection of social reform as a legitimate
sphere for religious activity by many evangelical leaders
and a concomitant overemphasis on individual piety. Sin
was seen as an individual affair to be dealt with on an
individual basis. Thus, attention was focused on personal
vice—alcoholic beverages, smoking, theater attendance,
prostitution, gambling, card playing—while social sin—
slums, poverty, political corruption, fraudulent business
practices, monopolies, hazardous working conditions,
adulteration of foods—was deliberately ignored or overlooked. The result was that a mood of indifference set-
tled over these churches as they withdrew from sociopolitical affairs and promoted the piety of the local
congregations in almost total unconcern about social
evils.

Still another significant factor in the decline of social
concern was the capture of the evangelical churches by
business interests. Successful businessmen occupied positions of power and prestige in the churches, and their
money went to build grand edifices and finance the
church programs. This had a subtle but devastating effect upon the ministry of the church. The plight of the
poor and the workingman was discreetly ignored, while
more and more effort was devoted to the great crusade

against Demon Rum. One of the few genuinely prophetic voices among the evangelicals of the turn of the century, B. Fay Mills, not only attacked the liquor traffic but also said there should be better care for the poor, and the church should be concerned about the physical welfare of all citizens in the cities. He specifically spoke out against self-seeking businessmen and the rich, big-city churches that had abdicated their social responsibilities, and finally he was forced out of evangelistic work by conservative ministers who had sold out to *laissez-faire* capitalism and the *status quo*.[21]

The impact of the wealthy businessmen could be seen in the activities of the great evangelists of the era, D. L. Moody and Billy Sunday. Moody was closely associated with the Philadelphia department-store magnate John Wanamaker and received substantial support from such captains of industry and finance as Cyrus McCormick, Philip Armour, Jay Cooke, Cornelius Vanderbilt II, and J. P. Morgan. These gentlemen could not complain when he said: "It is a wonderful fact that men and women saved by the blood of Jesus rarely remain subjects of charity, but rise at once to comfort and respectability"; or "I never saw the man who put Christ first in his life that wasn't successful." And naturally they would look with approval upon the words of instruction he gave his ministerial supporters in 1897: "Don't let Sunday be given up to talking on topics you don't understand such as capital and labor."[22]

Billy Sunday's record in this respect was even worse.

[21] McLoughlin, *Modern Revivalism: Charles Grandison Finney to Billy Graham* (New York: Ronald, 1959), pp. 338–44.

[22] Quoted in *ibid.*, pp. 252–53, 269. See Moody's recent definitive biography by James F. Findlay, Jr., *Dwight L. Moody: American Evangelist, 1837–1899* (Chicago: University of Chicago Press, 1969).

32 *The Unequal Yoke*

His principal business backer was John D. Rockefeller, Jr.,
while others contributing to his work included S. S.
Kresge, Elbert H. Gary, Louis F. Swift, Henry C. Frick,
and John M. Studebaker. A *New York Times* columnist
asserted that Sunday was supported by the well-to-do "as
a police measure—as a means of keeping the lower
classes quiet." [23] Alba B. Johnson, president of the Bald-
win Locomotive Works in Philadelphia, said:

> You know the widespread social unrest is largely due to
> the workingman's envy of those who make a little more
> money than he does. Now Billy Sunday makes people look
> to the salvation of their own souls, and when a man is
> looking after his own soul's good he forgets his selfish de-
> sire to become rich. Instead of agitating for a raise in
> wages he turns and helps some poorer brother who's down
> and out.[24]

The revivalists contributed significantly to spreading
the Gospel, but Bruce Shelley has accurately noted
that their practice of reducing the complexities of the
Christian faith to simple alternatives in order to call
men to make clear-cut decisions for Christ actually over-
simplified matters. To repent and believe was considered
all-important and following out the commandments of
Christ was not sufficiently stressed. Further, the tendency to emphasize results for result's sake, and to justify
whatever tended to produce them, subtly but definitely
diluted the good news of the Gospel.[25] In time new
elements crept into the evangelistic message such as the
middle-class success myth, American chauvinism, opposi-

[23] *The New York Times,* May 20, 1916, p. 10.
[24] Quoted in John Reed, "Back of Billy Sunday," *Metropolitan Magazine,* Vol. XLI (May, 1915), p. 12.
[25] Shelley, *op. cit.,* p. 52.

tion to actions of organized labor, and of course prohibition. Many revivalists were devoting as much effort to
outlawing saloons as to the winning of men to Jesus
Christ. Prohibition was the one reform issue that orthodox Christians could advocate without disturbing the
socioeconomic power structure, and soon it became the
solution for all the ills of society.

Extreme premillennial views also weakened evangelical social concern. Many Christians adopted an entirely
pessimistic outlook toward the present age. Until the
return of Christ, none of the basic problems of the world
could be solved. In 1914 Reuben A. Torrey stated: "In
the Return of our Lord is the perfect solution, and the
only solution, of the political and commercial problems
that now vex us." [26] Thus, human suffering was a sign of
the end of time, a necessary prelude to the coming of
Christ, and one could assume that conditions would
inevitably grow worse. Christians must devote all their
efforts to winning souls and preparing them for the afterlife. As one preacher crudely put it: "You don't polish
brass on a sinking ship."

The impact of these developments on twentieth-century evangelical Christianity has been subtle and far-
reaching. In the first place, many Christians concluded
that in order to "seek first the kingdom of God and his
righteousness" (Matthew 6:33) they should withdraw
into a shell of monastic pietism, concentrating exclu-
sively on their own spiritual lives and personal evangelism. Because the world could contaminate the individual believer, contacts were to be avoided as much as
possible, with the exception of occasional forays into
enemy territory to preach the Gospel. A doctrine of

[26] Quoted in McLoughlin, *Modern Revivalism*, p. 374.

individualism emerged that undermined the position of the church as the Christian community, emphasized noninvolvement with the problems of the world, and played directly into the hands of political rightism.[27] Where this would lead was clearly revealed in an editorial entitled "Christian Individualism" in the Radical Right publication, the *Dan Smoot Report:*

> The Christian concept of equality is spiritual. . . . It simply gives a little, imperfect man born in sin, an individual, personal relationship with God equal to that of any other man on earth. In short, Christianity exalts individualism, stressing the importance and exclusive dependence on God and self of the human individual.
>
> The strength and culture of America, built on faith in Jesus Christ, will start degenerating when Americans no longer hold aloft the central tenet of the Christian faith, namely, that the human individual (not the *masses* or *society*, but the *individual*) is a divinely important being, because God sent His only begotten Son into the world to make a blood atonement for the sins of individuals.[28]

Second, substantial segments of orthodox Protestantism became so closely identified with the *status quo* that they were blind to the evils of contemporary society. The material prosperity of modern times made many Christians lose interest in changing the world because they had a personal stake in preserving it as it was. One prominent Baptist minister, Russell H. Conwell, tickled the ears of the wealthy by lecturing around the country that financial success was a reflection of personal right-

---

[27] See the trenchant criticism of this by Henry Stob, "Fundamentalism and Political Rightism," *Reformed Journal*, Vol. XV (January, 1965), 12–14.

[28] *Dan Smoot Report*, Vol. XIII (December 25, 1967), pp. 206–07.

eousness while poverty was a mark of God's punishment.[29] Few leading evangelicals dared (or bothered) to speak out against the entrenched evil of segregation but instead soothingly told their white parishioners that black people needed "to be with their own kind." The church was the great stabilizer of American society, and God was employed as the servant of the vested interests of power and wealth.

Third, social action was seen as the province of individuals. The church or its leadership was forbidden to take the initiative in tackling current problems, either by making pronouncements or by direct intervention (charitable endeavors were regarded as a harmless and permissible exception!). Presbyterian Albert J. Lindsey told an N.A.E. convention that the Gospel "should motivate individuals to social action through the state." The church would present principles but should not endorse or give support to specific contemporary movements and organizations.[30] A prominent evangelical journalist, James DeForest Murch, declared: "The Church must not, as a corporate body, involve itself in economic, social and political affairs. Protestantism has always recognized the principle that Christians, as individuals, have the responsibility to involve themselves in these economic, social and political affairs for which they possess competence. The true purpose of the Church is to regenerate man." [31] Thus, the ministry of the church is salvific, not prophetic, and it should restrict its activities to the ecclesiastical realm.

[29] *Acres of Diamonds* (New York: Harper & Brothers, 1915).

[30] Albert J. Lindsey, "The Church and Social Action," *United Evangelical Action*, Vol. XVII (July 15, 1958), p. 4.

[31] Murch, *The Protestant Revolt: Road to Freedom for American Churches* (Arlington, Va.: Crestwood Books, 1967), p. 82.

Of course, this view neglects the rather obvious point that born-again Christians remain noticeably sinful and might very well make themselves and their interests the center of reference for their actions. This leads to a fourth item, namely, that those who desired the maintenance of the *status quo* were (and still are) vocal proponents of the individualistic approach to social action. For example, wealthy manufacturer and Baptist layman W. Maxey Jarman wrote that the early church "did not mount crusades to reform the general citizenry. In their day there was much wickedness in the world, as there is now, but they were concerned about the discipline of their own members, not about a universal welfare program." [32] Congregationalist minister Norman Read insisted that it is "the business of the clergyman and of the church to build religiously oriented individuals with strong moral character and send them out into the world to transform that world into something more akin to the Kingdom of God," but at the same time said that he despises "socialism in all of its forms, whether it be called the New Deal, the Fair Deal, the New Frontier, or the Great Society." [33] One of the most powerful political conservatives who at the same time is intimately identified with evangelical Christianity, multimillionaire oilman J. Howard Pew, remarked in two widely distributed magazines that "the corporate church should not speak outside its ecclesiastical sphere," and:

Christ himself made a clear distinction between the concerns of temporal and spiritual natures. . . . At no time

[32] W. Maxey Jarman, *A Businessman Looks at the Bible* (Westwood, N.J.: Revell, 1965), p. 119.

[33] Norman S. Read, "A Clergyman Looks at Free Enterprise," *The Freeman*, Vol. XVI (August, 1966), pp. 30, 26.

did he countenance civil disobedience or promote political pressure either to correct social evils or to advance his spiritual mission. His highest priority was given to measures for changing the hearts of men and women, knowing full well that changed men and women would in time change society—as indeed they have done all down the ages. He made it crystal-clear that we are to seek "first the kingdom of God and His righteousness"—carefully pointing out that "the kingdom is within you." [34]

Affinities Between Biblical Christianity and Political Conservatism

Dr. Carl McIntire once said the idea that "Christianity does not support any particular social system" is a deception which must be ascribed to sin.[35] Clearly he feels there is a biblical basis for a social system which he proceeds to label "capitalism." What Scriptural arguments, then, are conservatives able to marshal in support of their position?

The starting point is almost invariably the Ten Commandments (Exodus 20:1–17). The First Commandment, "You shall have no other gods before me," downgrades the power of the state. Since man is responsible above all to God, he must be free from absolute control by any human organism. This rules out collectivism because that exalts the state over God. The commandment regarding the Sabbath instituted the principle of a regu-

[34] J. Howard Pew, "Social Issues and Politics: Are Churches Going Too Far?" *U.S. News and World Report*, Vol. XLVIII (April 25, 1960), p. 135; "Should the Church 'Meddle' in Civil Affairs?" *Readers Digest*, Vol. LXXXVIII (May, 1966), p. 53.

[35] Carl McIntire, *"Author of Liberty"* (Collingswood, N.J.: Christian Beacon, 1946), p. 160.

lar time of rest and worship for all men. To honor one's
parents means that we must learn all we can from our
parents, ancestors, and history, and thereby profit by the
accumulated wisdom of the race. The ban on murder
fosters harmonious human relationships and is the dike
that holds back savagery. The precept concerning adultery supports the integrity of the home and family,
which is the basic institution of society. "You shall not
steal" both prohibits personal theft and signifies that no
state or legislature has the right to take the fruits of one's
labor. The commandment about false witness enshrines
honesty in human relationships and evaluates truthful-
ness to an exalted status even in relations among states.
The injunction against covetousness means that a person
has no right to demand what his neighbor possesses and
definitely forbids such schemes as equalization of wealth
or the progressive income tax.[36]

There are a number of other biblical concepts that
conservatives endeavor to draw upon. The doctrine of sin
stressed that human beings are not essentially good and
therefore the restrictions of the moral law must be en-
forced. This stands in opposition to a permissive society
where moral strictures are relaxed and the person is given
whatever he wants. The divine absolutes (such as divine
justice) are cast in the either-or mold so characteristic of
conservative thinking. In moral questions there is no
middle way. God, not the voice of majorities, will carry
the day. The New Testament stress on individual salvation and the proclamation of the Gospel to individuals is
taken to justify political, economic, and social individu-

[36] This approach to the Decalogue is found throughout conservative
writings. One of the most lucid presentations is in Howard E. Kershner,
God, Gold and Government (Englewood Cliffs, N.J.: Prentice-Hall,
1957), pp. 43–49.

alism. The voluntarism of Christianity is also appealed to by conservatives: has not the church, from its very beginning, done its own welfare work—regardless of the actions of the state? Individuals will change the world through their godly lives, as they practice such biblical virtues as initiative, industry, and self-reliance. Obedience to the moral law is rendered willingly and joyously, and must not be forced upon Christians by the state!

Of course, conservatives have their favorite proof texts. For example, in Luke 12:13–15 Christ refused to get involved in the division of an inheritance (a question of wealth); hence—the interpretation goes—there should be no compulsion to redistribute wealth and equalize income. In Matthew 26:11 Jesus declared that "you always have the poor with you," which means, we are told, that the welfare state or the war on poverty violates God's moral order. In the Beatitudes the poor are blessed of God, thus suggesting that God (not man) should take care of their needs in due time. Acts 4:32–37 is seen as an attempt on the part of the early church to establish a collectivist economy—an attempt that failed miserably and was discontinued because it was bound up with lying, as evidenced by Ananias and Sapphira. Paul taught that those who did not work should not be allowed to eat, that is, to live off the labors of other Christians (II Thessalonians 3:10). Surely this condemns the welfare state!

The danger of the Unequal Yoke with political conservatism is that it distorts the relationship of evangelical Christianity to contemporary American culture. The church has allowed itself to become so identified with the upper and middle classes that it is rapidly losing the opportunity to communicate the Gospel effectively to the lower classes and minority groups. Further, many "over thirty" evangelicals are finding it difficult to influence their own children because young people quickly recognize the difference between theological profession and actual deeds. Culbert Rutenber wisely points out that if the church refuses to relate itself positively to the social struggle, its very existence will be in peril. He adds:

Where the Church refuses to offer Christian leadership to the masses, Satan raises up his own, which proceeds to muffle the voice of the Church to a whisper. This is the lesson of the totalitarian state. A Church that is negatively related to the struggles of history can neither be salt nor light to the world.[37]

[37] Culbert G. Rutenber, *The Dagger and the Cross: An Examination of Christian Pacifism* (Nyack, N.Y.: Fellowship, 1958), p. 128.

II The Parasites of the Far Right

I appeal to you, brethren, to take note of those who create dissensions and difficulties, in opposition to the doctrine which you have been taught; avoid them. For such persons do not serve our Lord Christ, but their own appetites, and by fair and flattering words they deceive the hearts of the simple-minded. (Romans 16:17–18)

Listen, my beloved brethren. Has not God chosen those who are poor in the world to be rich in faith and heirs of the kingdom which he has promised to those who love him? But you have dishonored the poor man. Is it not the rich who oppress you, is it not they who drag you into court? Is it not they who blaspheme that honorable name by which you are called? (James 2:5–7)

For any self-respecting person, any person who loves his country and fears God, there is no such thing as the middle of the road. A special place in hell is being reserved for people who believe in walking down the middle of the political and religious road. It will be their privilege to fry with Eleanor Roosevelt and Adlai Stevenson. (The Rev. David Noebel, Christian Crusade) [1]

The radical right today is an even deadlier threat to our democratic traditions and institutions than are American adherents to communism. . . . They continue to peddle their poisonous package of defective and dangerous goods, hoodwinking honest but uninformed Americans with the sweet elixir of an easy cure for complex problems. In an effort to delude Americans they call their product conservatism, but it is a contaminated conservatism that would conserve nothing, but would destroy and devour basic democratic institutions. (Senator Stephen Young) [2]

What Is the Radical Right?

The existence of a rather variegated body of adherents to ultraconservative positions provides evangelical Christianity with an extremely serious problem for the reason that the vast majority of them regard themselves as devout Christians. They closely identify their cause with that of Christianity, as evidenced by a statement of Billy James Hargis: "Christ is the heart of the Conservative cause. We conservatives are fighting for God and Country." [3] Radical Rightists direct their appeals to conservative Christians and solicit financial support from them. The apparent affinities between orthodox Christi-

[1] From a sermon given in a Baptist church in Lansdale, Pa., quoted in Pete Martin, "I Call on Billy James Hargis," *Christian Herald*, Vol. XC (February, 1967), p. 20.

[2] *Congressional Record*, 88th Cong., 1st Sess., 1963, Vol. CIX, Part 11, pp. 15178–9.

[3] *Christian Crusade*, Vol. XIV (October, 1962), p. 14, quoted in John H. Redekop, *The American Far Right: A Case Study of Billy James Hargis and Christian Crusade* (Grand Rapids, Mich.: Eerdmans, 1968), p. 43.

anity and the Extreme Right have led one prominent historian to make the sweeping but inaccurate generalization that "the new evangelicals are the spiritual hardcore of the radical right." [4]

It is not really accurate to regard the Radical Right as synonymous with responsible conservatism as left-wing commentators often are guilty of doing. There are, to be sure, areas of similarity; Far Right spokesmen would readily agree to the definition of conservatism in the previous chapter. Both Rightists and conservatives speak for the privileged classes in American society, they are firmly committed to American nationalism, limited government, and the preservation of property rights, and they have a built-in resistance to change, particularly rapid change. Due to these similarities of viewpoint contacts often exist between responsible conservatives and the Far Right, and some well-meaning conservatives have injudiciously lent their names, endorsement, and financial support to organizations and causes of the Radical Right, even though they may not have been fully in sympathy with these.

However, the differences are significant and should be underscored. First, the Far Right views the communist menace in absolute terms. Thus, while conservatives attribute such things as the movement toward socialism in the United States or "softness" in dealing with communist regimes to blindness, stupidity, and bungling on the part of liberals who have been in control of the American government, Far Rightists see these as resulting from a sinister plot in high places, a "communist conspiracy." Because of this conspiratorial interpretation of history the Rightist is committed to immediate and direct ac-

[4] McLoughlin, *Daedalus*, p. 61.

tion to defeat the communist foe. Politics is the arena in which he struggles with the enemy, and he dares not stop short of complete and total victory. Hence, he cannot conceive of the possibility of a legitimate opposition but rather will use every tactic available even if some of these might stand outside the framework of American democratic procedures. He rejects the political system and the give-and-take of political compromise as a circus which diverts the people from the true issues. Further, the Extreme Rightist not only denounces governmental action to deal with social problems, but also he denies that the problems even exist and therefore has no alternative plans of action to suggest. In fact, the Rightist is reactionary, in that he has no desire to conserve much of what the liberals have introduced into American social, economic, and political life. He wishes to return to the kind of society which he feels existed before the advocates of big government had tampered with it.[5]

There are some common denominators among adherents to the Radical Right that can be identified. The unifying factor is an intense, active anticommunism in which the life-and-death nature of the struggle overshadows everything else. The Red conspiracy is evident everywhere, and the Rightist endeavors to fight it on all fronts. Although the external threat is not completely ignored, the primary emphasis is invariably placed on combating the domestic enemy, and direct action is the means to gain victory. A second denominator is a full-blown individualism in social, economic, and political relationships. This is reflected in rejection of state-supported welfare programs, advocacy of free-enterprise capitalism, and opposition to "big government." American

[5] Redekop, *op. cit.*, pp. 188–89.

patriotism is exalted as the defense against internationalism which is part of the communist conspiracy. Third, a generally negative and pessimistic tone pervades the Far Right. The victory of the enemy seems almost inevitable because the key decision makers cannot be made aware of the gravity of the Red menace. The Rightists have little or no positive program for social advancement which they can offer. A fourth characteristic is a common pattern of leadership. Usually heading up Rightist groups are such people as small-town evangelists, the newly rich, retired military officers, and persons who have been involved professionally in subversive activities such as former FBI agents, counterespionage men, and ex-communists. Also, most extremists manifest a strong strain of anti-intellectualism and emphasize emotion rather than reason. A person need not have any credentials to be an expert on public affairs, and those who do are frequently looked down upon as "eggheads." A sixth common factor is a tendency toward simplism. People, ideas, and events are seen in stark black-and-white, either-or terms. The Rightist falls back on firm, stereotyped views that permit no ambivalence or half-measures. Finally, such people manifest a deep sense of hostility, particularly to ideological enemies. They generally feel threatened and alienated and thus direct hate and aggression toward their foes. This accounts for the unethical and even violent behavior on the part of many ultraconservatives.

The tactics used by Radical Right extremists should be carefully noted. One is the formation of tightly organized groups which enable them to bring pressure to bear on the community power structures. Another tactic is that of infiltrating and gaining control of existing organizations such as political parties, civic and service clubs, school boards, PTAs, and churches. This may be accomplished by prolonging meetings until most people have left and then having measures adopted which support the Rightist position or by electing their people to key positions. A third form of action is the conscious fostering of distrust of community leaders. Elected officials, teachers, churchmen, and such people may be accused of being active communist agents or dupes of the communist line, and thus suspicion is raised as to their patriotism or loyalty, even though no concrete evidence is actually presented. A most dangerous tactic is that of coercion or even intimidation. This may be in the form of letter-writing campaigns, telephone calls, economic boycott, heckling and harassment at meetings, name calling and wanton smears, whispering campaigns, and even violence such as shootings or bombings.

Why did the Radical Right experience such a resurgence in the 1950's and 1960's? Political scientist John H. Redekop suggests a number of reasons growing out of a deep sense of national frustration. The major precipitant of this was communism which, because of its elusive nature, incomprehensibility, and newness of methodology, put its opponents on the defensive. The problem was accentuated by the American practice of infusing patriotism and nationalism with a sense of moral righteousness, resulting in the ideology of Americanism. The traditional values of America seemed to be under great attack by communism, and each international crisis only strengthened the Far Right by aggravating its fears and frustrations—Korea, Indochina, Hungary, and naturally the humiliation of the Sputnik launching. The victory of Castro in Cuba, more than anything else, resulted in the crystallization of the Radical Right. On the domestic scene conservatives grew increasingly dissatisfied with

continued deficit spending, growing federal power, foreign-aid expenditures, the Supreme Court decision on
school desegregation in 1954, and the failure to adopt an
aggressive foreign policy toward communist regimes, especially the Soviet Union and Cuba. The unwillingness
of American liberals to manifest the same type of hostility toward totalitarian communism in the postwar years
that they had toward fascism in the 1930's left conservatives bewildered and disturbed. Many Americans, frus-
trated by the problems of world leadership, the communist threat, and the lack of some meaningful ideological
mooring in modern society, turned to the Far Right.
Added to this was a religious dimension, a revitalized
fundamentalism, which seemed to be naturally allied to
the emerging Rightist ideology of Americanism.[6]

Until recently, evangelicals have been reticent to
speak out in ringing terms against the activities of the
extremists on the right because of a basic sympathy with
their conservative objectives and a mistaken understanding of the nature of their Christian faith. With a few
exceptions—such as Donald Grey Barnhouse's incisive
examination of the Air Force Manual controversy in
1960, articles by Don Hillis and the present author in
1962 questioning the anticommunist mania which had
gripped many evangelical churches, the special issue of
the *Reformed Journal* in January, 1965, dealing with the
Far Right, and the forthright analysis of the John Birch
Society by Lester DeKoster in the same year—evangelical
publications until very recently were strangely silent or
for the most part equivocal on the matter of the Radical
Right.[7] At the very same time there was a spate of litera-

[6] *Ibid.*, pp. 142–51.
[7] Donald Grey Barnhouse, "Communism and the National Council
of Churches: An Impartial Investigation of Charges Made by the

ture in the secular and liberal Protestant press on the topic. Some evangelicals who did denounce Extreme Rightist activities were subjected to vilification. For example, when Frank H. Bellinger, a political science professor at Wheaton College, published an article in the Wheaton alumni magazine which contained some criticisms of the John Birch Society, he became the object of intense harassment by one of the college's alumni, while Mark Hatfield's courageous remarks about Radical Rightist bigotry in his keynote address at the Republican National Convention on July 13, 1964, resulted in an outpouring of invective. One woman who labeled herself a "Bible-believing Baptist" told the then governor of Oregon that he showed "a lack of Christian discernment and responsibility to the truth." [8] The unwillingness of much of evangelical Christianity to face up to the menace of the Radical Right is most unfortunate, for the Rightists are parasites feeding on the lifeblood of the church and sapping the strength of its witness.

Christian Rightism

Most of the critical literature on the Radical Right seeks to explain the movement in terms of psychological problems and personality traits, sociological factors such

Controversial Air Force Manual," *Eternity*, Vol. XI (September, 1960), pp. 6–9; Don W. Hillis, "Should the Church Fight Communism?" *United Evangelical Action*, Vol. XXI (April, 1962), pp. 17–18; Richard V. Pierard, "The Problem of Anti-communism," *The Standard*, Vol. LII (August 20, 1962), p. 27; "Special Supplement on the Far Right," *Reformed Journal*, Vol. XV (January, 1965), pp. 11–31; Lester DeKoster, *The Christian and the John Birch Society* (Grand Rapids, Mich.: Eerdmans, 1965).
[8] *The New York Times*, July 15, 1964, p. 22.

as socioeconomic dislocation and status anxiety, and the frustrations and fears which abound in American society. Less attention has been paid to the religious side of the Far Right, and much that has been written comes from authors unsympathetic to conservative Christianity.[9] An evangelical treatment of Billy James Hargis noted quite correctly that one of the most important shortcomings of the works on the Far Right "is the widespread failure to evaluate the significance of Christian fundamentalism, or even orthodox Christianity, as a contributing factor, especially in conjunction with traditional American-ism."[10]

Orthodox Christianity in itself does not produce Extreme Rightism but, as noted in the previous chapter, it has frequently been forced to yield proof texts for it. The Rightist conception of life as a struggle between absolute good and absolute evil can be reinforced by such Scriptural citations (conveniently removed from context) as: "I know your works: you are neither cold nor

[9] Examples of this include David Danzig, "The Radical Right and the Rise of the Fundamentalist Minority," *Commentary*, Vol. XXXIII (April, 1962), pp. 291–98; Raymond E. Wolfinger and others, "America's Radical Right: Politics and Ideology," in David E. Apter, *Ideology and Discontent* (New York: Free Press, 1964); Brooks R. Walker, *The Christian Fright Peddlers* (Garden City, N.Y.: Doubleday, 1964); and Arnold Forster and Benjamin Epstein, *Danger on the Right* (New York: Random House, 1964).

[10] Redekop, *op. cit.*, p. 9. Two other recent works that stress the significance of Christianity in understanding the Extreme Right are Pierard, "Christianity, Democracy, and the Radical Right," in Robert G. Clouse, Robert L. Linder, and Richard V. Pierard, eds., *Protest and Politics: Christianity and Contemporary Affairs* (Greenwood, S.C.: Attic Press, 1968), pp. 38–64; and Erling Jorstad, *The Politics of Doomsday: Fundamentalists of the Far Right* (Nashville, Tenn.: Abingdon, 1970). The thorough and perceptive study by Jorstad appeared just as this book went to press, and thus it was impossible to make use of his insights.

hot. Would that you were cold or hot! So, because you are lukewarm, and neither cold nor hot, I will spew you out of my mouth" (Revelation 3:15–16). The biblical view of a world divided into the saved and the lost leaves no room for middle ground, and this can easily be transferred by false analogy into terms of an apocalyptic conflict between Christianity and communism as a life-and-death struggle in which compromise is inconceivable.

The role of "hate" in Christianity is also significant. The believer is repeatedly instructed to despise sin and evil. "Hate evil and love good" (Amos 5:15). "The Lord loves those who hate evil" (Psalm 97:10). "The fear of the Lord is hatred of evil" (Proverbs 8:13). "Thou hatest all evildoers. Thou destroyest those who speak lies" (Psalm 5:5–6). An attitude of intolerance toward genuine moral evil can easily be shifted to political issues. Communism is the catch-all for everything undesirable in modern urban society, from sexual immodesty to permissive child-rearing practices, and by equating it with sin and atheism as the Rightist does, he can easily enlist the moral fervor of Christians in a crusade for righteousness and against evil.

The doctrine of Satan is employed to lend credence to the conspiratorial view of the Rightist. The biblical teaching about the devil as the "ruler of this world" (John 12:31) and "an angel of light" (II Corinthians 11:14) provides the basis for belief in a "control apparatus" of evil. Satan is omnipresent and continually active in subverting the purposes of God in the world, and the Christian is urged to beware of the "wiles of the devil" (Ephesians 6:11) and the "snare of the devil" (II Timothy 2:26). This makes the omnipresence of the communist conspiracy plausible! Because Satan is so cunning,

even such seemingly beneficial movements as political
liberalism and socialism are nothing but camouflages
which conceal the communist realities from the unwary
believer. As Carl McIntire said: " 'The government that
does the most for its people is the best' is a most subtle
form of Satanic propaganda." [11] Every move of the ad-
versary is carefully planned to bring about the ultimate
aim of communism, and the committed Christian must
always be on the alert to fend off the assaults of Satan.

The association between the Protestant work ethic
and the ideology of nineteenth-century capitalism contributes to the extreme individualism of the Rightist.
Conservative Protestants generally have stressed individual initiative and the related values of prudence, dili-
gence, thrift, self-reliance, and industry, and one is re-
warded for virtue and hard work and punished for vice
and indolence. Thus, the government has no responsibility for meeting the physical needs of its citizens or recti-
fying seeming social and economic injustices. Every individual is a divinely created sovereign, made in the image
of God, and capable of determining his own wants and
satisfying them in the open marketplace. The government has no business tampering with these "God-given
rights" because such action would prevent the individual
from developing his full potential and shaping his own
destiny. Of course, not all will succeed but what a person
does is his own responsibility.[12] That this article of faith
is nothing but a crude social Darwinism seems to escape
both the Christian and the Rightist.

Commentators frequently assume that "religious fundamentalism and Radical Rightism just naturally go in

[11] McIntire, *"Author of Liberty,"* p. 163.
[12] Redekop, *op. cit.*, pp. 136–37.

tandem," but this is not accurate. It is more correct to say that the Far Right misrepresents Christianity by advancing a doctrine which mixes with alien elements those aspects of the New Testament that relate to personal salvation and those of the Old Testament that stress Israel's uniqueness.[13] In addition, the Extreme Right has taken over the revivalistic techniques of American Protestantism, and so a rally or "crusade" with its singing of stirring religious and patriotic hymns, passionate appeals for funds, and haranguing, fright-inducing sermons takes on the appearance of an old-fashioned revival meeting. Far Rightists actually distort evangelical Christianity and appropriate its doctrines, techniques, and emotional fervor for their own ends.

Christian Organizations on the Far Right

Literally hundreds of right-of-center organizations have been identified, many of which could be labeled as Far Right in nature. At least two dozen of these have made a significant national impact, the best known being the John Birch Society. A study in 1964 revealed that these groups were spending a minimum of $14 million annually, with the major portion coming from tax-exempt foundations, business firms and corporations, and well-to-do businessmen.[14] Also, a sizable amount was raised from ordinary citizens by means of dues, collections at meetings, mail solicitation, and sale of propaganda material. Nearly all spokesmen of the Extreme Right profess to have religious faith and emphasize the

[13] Harry and Bonaro Overstreet, *The Strange Tactics of Extremism* (New York: Norton, 1964), p. 145.
[14] Forster and Epstein, *op. cit.*, pp. 272–77.

importance of Christianity in American history and society. Moreover, certain Rightist organizations specifically claim to be "Christian" in their nature and basic
thrust. These will be pointed out so that the reader can
be made aware of them and the manner in which they
prey upon churches and concerned Christians for funds
and support. Evangelicals should take note of them and
avoid them (Romans 16:17).

The Christian Anti-Communism Crusade, headed by
Dr. Frederick C. Schwarz, specializes in alerting Americans to the dangers of communism. Schwarz, an Austra-
lian-born medical doctor, became an avid student of
communist ideology in the 1940's. He was brought to
the United States by the American Council of Christian
Churches and in 1953 set up his own organization. He
said that he took up the struggle against communism
because "I was an evangelical Christian and the Communists are evangelical in another sense. I knew they
intend to destroy what I stood for. I am not ashamed to
say that I am a narrow-minded, Bible-believing Baptist.
On that basis is built my Crusade." [15] An appearance
before the House Un-American Activities Committee in
1957 suddenly elevated him into a figure of national
repute. His testimony was published as a government
document and later expanded into a book entitled *You
Can Trust the Communists (to Be Communists)* [16]
which appeared in 1960. Although the book was a woefully simplistic treatment of communism, it experienced
a wide distribution (nearly a million copies) in a paper-
back edition. The high point was reached in 1961 when
the Christian Anti-Communism Crusade reported to the

[15] Quoted in Mark Sherwin, *The Extremists* (New York: St. Martin's, 1963), p. 119.
[16] Englewood Cliffs, N.J.: Prentice-Hall, 1960.

Internal Revenue Service an income in excess of one
million dollars, and its Hollywood Bowl rally got
extensive television coverage. Since then, Schwarz's pop-
ularity has waned appreciably and his income has
dropped off. He has, however, had a notable measure of
support from respectable people, particularly Patrick J.
Frawley, Jr., president of Schick Safety Razor Company.

The organization assists in the establishment of anticommunist study groups in communities, distributes
substantial quantities of anticommunist printed materi-
als and tape recordings, and sponsors weekend seminars
and rallies. It is best known, however, for its anticommunist "schools." A school is held in a large metropolitan area, when possible, and normally lasts about five
days. It consists of an intensive program of lectures and
films during a twelve-hour day with time out for meals,
where students have ample opportunity to discuss what
they have learned and how they can effectively combat
communism, and the week is climaxed by a gala ban-
quet. Schwarz is the chief lecturer and quite effectively
communicates his views to the students who have paid
"tuition" to attend the school. He sticks rather faithfully
to the central theme that he is leading a Christian crusade to battle the atheistic conspiracy against Western
civilization, and restricts his lectures to communist philosophy and tactics. Schwarz definitely makes no anti-
Semitic appeal and does not personally engage in the
familiar Rightist game of finding governmental institutions honeycombed with communists and accusing the
highest American officials of treason. Unfortunately, he
makes no effort to exercise control over the "faculty"
(the other speakers) at his schools who, he contends,
have "academic freedom." This results in the opening of
a veritable Pandora's box of extremist ideas on the plat-
form as the "faculty members," which include such lu-

minaries in the Rightist firmament as Herbert Philbrick, Richard Arens, W. Cleon Skousen, William P. Strube, and Walter Judd, lash out against American foreign and domestic policy, the Supreme Court, desegregation, the United Nations, foreign aid, labor unions, the academic community, and other phobias of the Far Right. Moreover, Schwarz himself asserts repeatedly that, unless drastic changes occur in the policies and attitudes of the free world, the communists will conquer the United States by 1973. One scholarly study of conservative organizations in the United States observed that "The general effect of a Schwarz school is to create a sense of profound uneasiness toward, and a lack of confidence in, the present governmental leaders and their policies without elucidating any specific alternative policies. . . . He comes simply as a John the Baptist in reverse—as a 'bearer of bad tidings.' " [17]

Christian Crusade, founded and directed by an ordained minister in the Christian Church (Church of Christ), Billy James Hargis, is a distinctly different organization from that of Fred Schwarz and should not be confused with it. Raised in a poverty-stricken, fundamentalist home in the South, Hargis had only one and one-half years of college education before entering the ministry. In 1947, at the age of twenty-two, he dedicated himself to the cause of fighting communism. He saw this as central to the Christian Gospel and worked out a tightly knit creed combining Americanism, Christian fundamentalism, free enterprise, and anticommunism.[18] From the very beginning the group which he founded,

---

[17] Barbara Green and others, "Responsible and Irresponsible Right-Wing Groups: A Problem in Analysis," *Journal of Social Issues,* Vol. XIX (April, 1963), p. 16.

[18] Redekop, *op. cit.,* p. 17. My account of the Christian Crusade is based primarily on this excellent study.

Christian Crusade, was above all anticommunist. It grew
from an inconsequential local effort to an important
national organization largely through the personal dyna-
mism of Hargis.

It sponsored a diversified pattern of enterprises and
attracted a large number of prominent right-wingers to
its ranks. In some years the group's income approached
the million dollar mark, but its fund-raising activities
were definitely crippled by widespread attacks in the
mass media during the early 1960's and the revocation of
its tax-exempt status in 1966 for allegedly engaging in
political activities. Hargis' most significant outlet has
been his radio programs. Daily and weekly broadcasts
blanket the nation from between 400 and 450 stations.
Publications are another important enterprise. The
monthly *Christian Crusade* has a circulation of 120,000,
while pamphlets and books flow from the pens of Hargis
and his associates in an unending stream. A vast quantity
of miscellaneous items such as record albums, tape recordings, pictures, American flags, and reproductions of
historic documents are also sold from the ultramodern
Tulsa, Oklahoma, office. A few years ago the organization purchased an old resort hotel in Manitou Springs,
Colorado, and converted it into the "Anti-Communist
Youth University." "Christian Conservative" high-
school students and recent graduates are given two-week
summer courses in the Bible, free-enterprise system,
Constitutional government, and how to organize chapters of the anticommunist youth group, the Torchbear-
ers, in high schools and colleges. Hargis is president, his
assistant and youth specialist David Noebel is dean, and
military notables and prominent conservative spokesmen
serve as lecturers at the "university." Further, the anticommunist evangelist attracts considerable attention

with his annual Christian Crusade conventions in Tulsa each August, and at the 1969 meeting the third-party Presidential candidate George C. Wallace publicly endorsed Hargis and urged people to support his work.[19] Lately, Hargis has become deeply involved in the campaign against sex education in the public schools, and this has given him a new measure of national notoriety. Although critics repeatedly accuse the Tulsa Crusader of "being in it for the money," it is probably more correct to say that his primary motivation is an ever-growing Messiah complex. In reality he is a zealot, a man with a mission to save America from the vast horde of evils which he groups under one catch-all term, "communism."

The *Christian Freedom Foundation* is an organization of the Far Right which seeks to rally support for libertarian economic philosophies. It was established in 1950 by Howard E. Kershner, a respected Quaker humanitarian who had rejected the pacifist aspect of his religious heritage and had been a long-time critic of liberalism and the New Deal. The principal activity of the group is the publication of a biweekly four-page tabloid newspaper, *Christian Economics*, which is distributed free of charge to approximately 200,000 Protestant clergy and lay people in the United States. It also circulates a syndicated column entitled "It's Up to You" to several hundred newspapers, and has in the past produced a news-commentary radio program. Data published in the Anti-Defamation League study of the Far Right confirmed what many people had long suspected, namely, that Presbyterian layman J. Howard Pew regularly contributes the major portion of the finances required by the

[19] *The New York Times*, August 3, 1969, p. 48.

foundation.[20] Moreover, a founder and vice-president of the group until his death in May, 1969, was Dr. Frederick Curtis Fowler, a Presbyterian clergyman who served as president of the N.A.E. in 1950–52.

The main thrust of *Christian Economics* is that the Christian system is a free economic order with the least possible amount of government interference and regulation. Communism is a godless economic system and must be combated with a "God-centered economics," that is, *laissez-faire* capitalism. Communists are bad, anti-God people; capitalists are good, pro-God people. Because anything that is not capitalistic is communistic, there can be no middle ground, and all degrees and shades of collectivists are *ipso facto* communists. Howard Kershner believes that the "laws of economics are part of the laws of God," thus inferring that the farther a society moves from a completely free and unregulated economic order, the more it is rebelling against the authority of God and the teachings of the Christian faith. In short, *Christian Economics* espouses a religion that says *no* to the things of this world while at the same time adopting an economic philosophy that says *yes* to the world. The assumption is made that correct religion will bring material rewards and success in this life—God smiles on the capitalist and rewards him. Further, the survival of the church depends on the survival of capitalism. The unthinkable alternative is anti-God communism which will destroy the church at once should it ever gain power.[21]

The *Church League of America* directs its efforts to-

[20] Forster and Epstein, *op. cit.*, p. 268.
[21] Robert McAfee Brown, "Is It 'Christian Economics'?" *Christianity and Crisis*, Vol. X (November 27, 1950), pp. 155–58; Ralph Lord Roy, *Apostles of Discord* (Boston: Beacon, 1953), pp. 294–98.

ward subversive activities in the churches and assisting the clergy in opposing these dangerous tendencies. It was founded in 1937 by George Washington Robnett, a Chicago advertising agent, to carry on "an educational program designed to bring the influence of the clergy and educators more solidly behind the laymen in . . . their common ideal of preserving Constitutional rights and the basic traditions of the American Way of Life." [22] In order to carry out this task, the Church League initiated the publication of a monthly newsletter, *News and Views*, to give information about the leftist movement in the United States and in addition issues a number of "special reports" on this topic. The group operated on a shoestring budget as a minor right-wing educational organization until 1956 when Edgar C. Bundy took the helm. The new leader had served as an Air Force intelligence officer during World War II, and after returning to civilian life he remained in the reserve where he eventually attained the rank of major. Although he was ordained as a Southern Baptist minister in 1942, he never held a pastorate but rather worked as a newspaperman in Wheaton, Illinois. He gained fame as an expert on communism after accurately predicting developments in the Far East in testimony given before the Senate Appropriations Committee in 1949. He was associated with the American Council of Christian Churches for a brief period and was active in right-wing organizations in Illinois before assuming the leadership of the Church League of America. Its reputation grew rapidly after this time, and soon it ranked among the most important of the Christian Rightist groups.

The most noteworthy part of the Church League's

[22] Quoted in Roy, *op. cit.*, p. 234.

work is the collection of data about subversives and the
sale of it to customers much in the manner of an ideological credit-reporting agency. It professes to have over one
million 3 x 5 cross-referenced index cards on individuals,
organizations, and publications which "have served the
Communist cause in the United States." These data are
placed in three categories: Communist Party members;
fellow travelers, party sympathizers or front-joiners; and
mere "dupes" of communism. This "evidence" of communist involvements is gathered from reports of government agencies by the Church League itself and collated
in these files. Financial contributors to the organization
(those who give a thousand dollars or more) can obtain
secret "background reports" on the "philosophy of life"
of individuals (such as a prospective employee or
speaker) which will protect against "radical infiltration." [23] The fact that the data on persons could very
well be inaccurate or irrelevant or that a background
report could do immeasurable harm to the reputation of
a person never seems to have occurred to Major Bundy.

Bundy is also the author of a widely distributed book
entitled *Collectivism in the Churches* which the Church
League published in 1958. It is a biting attack on the
National Council of Churches, based primarily on the
data in the aforementioned files, and is a clear indication
of how such information can and will be misused. Nevertheless, the editor of *United Evangelical Action*
praised the book for documenting "the methods by
which the destruction of America's basic liberties is
being carried on by the Council in the name of Social
progress," while a leading evangelical minister told the

[23] Described in *Schism*, Vol. I (Summer, 1969), p. 25; and Forster
and Epstein, *op. cit.*, p. 147.

1958 N.A.E. national convention that Bundy set forth "significant facts" in this "most provocative work." [24] Other activities of the Church League include maintenance of an extensive library on communism and left-wing organizations at its spacious Wheaton headquarters and the sponsoring of "counter-subversive seminars" around the country. Recently, Bundy has been making lecture tours in South Africa where he alerts already sympathetic audiences to the danger of "communist infiltration" in the churches there.[25] It is, however, fair to say that, although the Church League is a well-known organization, Bundy has not attracted as much national notoriety as Schwarz or Hargis, and the group has not been so well-endowed financially as theirs.

A Rightist organization that distinctly emphasizes compiling lists of "suspect" persons is the *Circuit Riders, Inc.* This group, headquartered in Cincinnati, Ohio, was formed in 1951 by thirty-three Methodist laymen who declared their intention to resist efforts to propagate socialism, communism, and all other "anti-American teachings" in their denomination. This was aimed at the left-leaning Methodist Federation for Social Action, but even though the federation was soon discredited, the Circuit Riders did not disband. Instead, its executive secretary, Myers G. Lowman, a partner in an air-conditioning firm, transformed it into a much more extremist organization than its founders originally intended. Lowman began examining the "leftist affiliations" of clergymen, not only Methodists but other faiths as well, and publishing "fully documented" lists of ministers which contain "items of public record" about their alleged

[24] *United Evangelical Action*, Vol. XVII (April 1, 1958), p. 4 (July 15, 1958), p. 4.
[25] *The New York Times*, November 13, 1966, p. 6.

subversive involvement. His first list was entitled "A Compilation of Public Records of 2,109 Methodist Ministers" (1956). Following this were compilations of the "public records" of 614 Presbyterian, 1,411 Episcopalian, and 660 Baptist clergymen, 450 rabbis, "42 percent" of Unitarian clergymen, 30 of the 95 people who worked on the translation of the Revised Standard Version of the Bible, 658 clergymen and laymen connected with the National Council of Churches, and 6,000 educators.[26]

The Overstreets show clearly that Lowman's lists are ambiguous, meaningless, and prove nothing about the clergymen surveyed. The compilations serve only to arouse suspicions about their loyalty and offer unscrupulous people a weapon which they can use against the current leadership and policies of their denominations. It comes as no surprise that Lowman's material is widely used by other organizations on the Christian Radical Right and that he is in great demand as a speaker at Rightist seminars and schools. In spite of this, evangelical leader James DeForest Murch lauds the Circuit Riders for alerting "thousands in all denominations concerning the dangers of NCC socialistic and communistic propaganda," and insists it is "one of the most effective deterrents of wholesale subversive advance" within the Methodist denomination.[27]

One of the most aggressive organizations contending for ultraconservatism with a strong Christian emphasis is the *National Education Program,* which operates from the campus of Harding College, a Church of Christ school in Searcy, Arkansas. The program is the creation of George S. Benson, a former missionary to China, who in 1936 at the age of thirty-eight was called to the presi-

---

[26] Overstreets, *op. cit.,* pp. 157–61.
[27] Murch, *Protestant Revolt,* pp. 96, 147.

dency of the tiny Arkansas school. Benson, a persuasive talker, began preaching a simple gospel of Americanism in his neighborhood that gradually attracted more and more attention. His speeches extolling the virtues of free enterprise made a deep impression on many industrialists, and soon corporation and foundation gifts were pouring in to the coffers of the National Education Program, which he created in 1948. In order to gain accreditation for Harding College he was compelled to separate the program from the school. However, the N.E.P. was provided with rent-free facilities at the college, and a number of people divided their services between the two, so there was no doubt in anyone's mind that the two were closely linked. The influx of donations from conservative businessmen rapidly transformed Harding into a well-endowed college with several sparkling new buildings while the N.E.P. never lacked funds to carry out its activities.

The National Education Program has in the subsequent years turned out a vast quantity of right-wing propaganda. This includes innumerable pamphlets, a high-school study outline on American citizenship, a newspaper column distributed free to over three thousand weekly papers, monthly reprints of the column shipped in bulk lots to business firms for distribution to their employees, and the *National Program Letter* which is sent to fifty thousand subscribers. The program also supplies speakers who travel around the country and address PTAs and civic groups on patriotism, free enterprise, and anticommunism, while annual "Freedom Forums" are held on the Harding campus to train people in resistance to the spread of socialism and communism. Moreover, radio and television programs, film strips, and motion pictures are produced in large quantities. By far the most famous N.E.P. film has been *Communism on the Map* which was shown to literally millions of people in the early 1960's and which stirred up a national controversy almost equal to the one over *Operation Abolition.* By a striking use of pink and red colors the film depicts the gradual communist takeover of the world, following closely the views that John Birch Society founder Robert Welch expressed in his *Blue Book.*[28] Benson's appeal is, to be sure, somewhat more academic and more directed to winning business support than that of the anticommunist evangelists, but is just as effective in spreading the Rightist gospel.

Presbyterian minister *Carl McIntire* is one of the most energetic figures on the Christian Far Right and has been associated with a large number of enterprises during the past thirty-five years. Born in 1906 and raised in the Midwest, he began his theological studies at Princeton Theological Seminary. There he became a disciple of J. Gresham Machen, and when his teacher broke with Princeton in 1929, McIntire went with him to establish Westminster Seminary. He worked with Machen in the struggle against modernism in the Presbyterian Church, and in 1936 the two were dismissed from the ministry for causing dissension and strife in the church. Critics of the General Assembly's action insist, however, that the real issue was doctrine, not discipline. They formed a new denomination, the Orthodox Presbyterian Church, but within a year McIntire founded his own Bible Presbyterian Church and another school, Faith Theological Seminary.[29] In 1941 he created the American Council of

[28] Forster and Epstein, *op. cit.,* p. 91.

[29] This propensity for fragmentation is one factor which distinguishes Rightists from the genuinely orthodox. In defense of Machen see Ned B. Stonehouse, *J. Gresham Machen: A Biographical Memoir* (Grand Rapids, Mich.: Eerdmans, 1955).

Christian Churches and in 1948 the International Council of Churches, which were to be conservative counterweights to the National and World Councils of Churches. In his view the latter were apostate bodies needing to be resisted in every way possible.

McIntire rapidly gained a reputation through his writing and speaking as a formidable figure on the Extreme Right. His church in Collingswood, New Jersey, became a beehive of activity in support of the many endeavors of its indefatigable pastor. Since 1936 he has been the editor of the *Christian Beacon*, a weekly newspaper which incessantly attacks liberal and moderate churchmen alike (including those in the National Association of Evangelicals) and warns the American people of the perils of collectivism and countless other evils in the social and economic realm. The same line is expressed in the many books and pamphlets which flow from his Christian Beacon Press, especially *"Author of Liberty"* (1946) and *Servants of Apostasy* (1955). In 1958 he went into large-scale radio broadcasting with the *Twentieth Century Reformation Hour* which is now being heard over five hundred stations. He also controls Shelton College, a small liberal-arts school, and in 1963 purchased a resort hotel in Cape May, New Jersey, which he renamed the Christian Admiral. The hotel serves as a summer conference center and is frequented by religious and secular luminaries of the Right.

Although he has had considerable difficulty through the years in holding his supporters together, McIntire has never moderated his message. If anything, as he grows older, he is becoming more extreme in his attacks upon the National and World Councils of Churches, the Roman Catholic Church, the Revised Standard Version of the Bible, the United Nations, civil-rights agita-

tion and legislation, foreign-aid programs, softness toward communism, and social and economic legislation.
However, his empire seems to be collapsing around him.
During the 1950's his Bible Presbyterians suffered a de-
bilitating split that practically destroyed the denomination. His mission board, the Independent Board of Presbyterian Foreign Missions, slipped out of his hands.
Shelton College had to give up its beautiful campus in
Ringwood, New Jersey, and was moved to the Christian
Admiral, only to face a determined effort by the state
educational authorities to close it down. In 1968 he lost
control of the American Council and recently the largest
denomination in the International Council withdrew, as
his ideological associates became increasingly resentful
of his dictatorial behavior.[30] The future for Dr. McIntire
seems dark indeed.

Although these are by far the most significant bodies
of the Christian Far Right, many others could be mentioned. The *American Council of Christian Laymen*,
formed in 1949 by Verne P. Kaub, a public-utilities
agent in Madison, Wisconsin, was at one time a prominent agency for the distribution of right-wing religious
propaganda. In recent years it has declined, and after his
death in 1964 it was absorbed by the American Council
of Churches. *Spiritual Mobilization*, the creation of a
conservative Congregationalist minister in Los Angeles,
James W. Fifield, and once the "most influential of the
clergy-oriented bastions of unrestrained individualism,"[31] is now quite inconsequential. In the 1950's its
organ, *Faith and Freedom*, spoke as strongly for the
libertarian gospel as *Christian Economics* did. Some

[30] *The New York Times*, September 15, 1969, p. 51.
[31] Roy, *op. cit.*, p. 286.

groups are flash-in-the-pan operations, such as *Christian Citizen* which was founded in a blaze of publicity by Denver real-estate developer Gerri von Frellick. It aimed at training "evangelical Christians" in the techniques of practical politics so that they could gain control of the local, state, and federal governments and combat the inclination of the "public to accept the inevitable success of communism in America."[32] Nothing more was heard of the venture.

The Lutheran Church-Missouri Synod has been plagued with Rightists as well. The Rev. Herman J. Otten in New Haven, Missouri, publishes a weekly paper, *Christian News*, which is modeled on the *Christian Beacon* and concentrates heavily on political and social questions from an ultraconservative stance. A similar publication, *Through to Victory*, emanates from the study of Lutheran pastor Paul Neipp in Ridgecrest, California. Among other Christian Rightist organs and groups are the following: *The Western Voice* (Englewood, Colorado), which was founded by the now deceased Harvey Springer, the "Cowboy Evangelist" and intimate of Carl McIntire, is noted for its extremely conservative line. The same is true for John R. Rice's venerable paper, *The Sword of the Lord*, now edited in Murfreesboro, Tennessee. *The Capital Voice* is a monthly newsletter edited by evangelist Dale Crowley in Washington, D.C., which discusses current political events from a right-wing religious standpoint. An anticommunist radio preacher who is beginning to gain a following is Dr. Steuart McBirnie. His program, *Voice of Americanism*, originates from Glendale, California, and is heard nationwide. Of course, one hardly needs to

[32] *The New York Times,* February 1, 1962, p. 23.

mention that fountainhead of Christian Rightist propaganda in Greenville, South Carolina, Bob Jones University. A quick glance through the latest *First National
Directory of "Rightist" Groups* would bring to light the
names of many other obscure Far Right organizations
and publications with a religious flavor.[33]

One category which has been excluded from this dis-
cussion of Christian Rightism is that of the racist-or-
iented groups. The best known of these anti-Semitic and
white-supremacist groups are the Christian Nationalist
Crusade of Gerald L. K. Smith and the Defenders of the
Christian Faith founded by the late Gerald B. Winrod.
Some publications in this vein are *The Cross and the
Flag* (Gerald Smith), *Common Sense* (published in
Union, New Jersey, and edited by Conde McGinley
until his death in 1963), the *National Christian News*
(St. Petersburg, Florida), and the *Pilgrim Torch* (Englewood, Colorado). The great majority of conservatives
repudiate these radical fringe groups, and they have vir-
tually no influence on the thinking of American evangelical Christians.

*The Christian Far Right—Nuisance
or Menace?*

The harm which the Radical Right does to American
democratic institutions has repeatedly been noted by
commentators. Hate and distrust have been injected into
American life, as evidenced by the numerous smears,
whispering campaigns, and even bombings of homes and

[33] *First National Directory of "Rightist" Groups, Publications and
Some Individuals in the United States (and Some Foreign Countries)*,
5th ed. (Los Angeles: Alert Americans Association, 1965).

churches. The Rightists are unwittingly undermining faith in civil liberties, the two-party system, and the integrity of elected officials, and they have made a mockery of American patriotism. Moreover, their pressures for a more bellicose foreign policy play into the hands of the military-industrial complex and lead the country down a perilous path that could result in national destruction.

But the Christian Rightists need to be singled out for special consideration. The Christian faith stresses such virtues as love for one's neighbor, selflessness, humility, and peacefulness, while the behavior of the Far Right utterly negates these. Liberal observers often look upon the Christian Rightists as harmless cranks, a lunatic element on the fringe of American Christianity, but it cannot be denied that they have inflicted untold damage on individual people and religious and community organizations. For instance, Howard and Arlene Eisenberg describe in graphic terms how Edgar Bundy destroyed a philosophy professor at a small Midwestern Christian college. When the youthful and conscientious educator set out to refute Bundy's innuendoes, the Church League's leader wrote an influential community pastor that the teacher was "a known Communist and poisoner of young people's minds." The letter eventually reached the college's president who immediately silenced the professor because he feared Bundy's attacks would bring about a reduction in giving that would harm the college financially.[34] Similar accounts could be related by anyone who has had extensive contacts with Extreme Rightists.

One of the most graphic examples of the damage Christian Far Rightists can do to the cause of Christ is a

[34] Howard and Arlene Eisenberg, "The Far Right and the Churches," *Progressive*, Vol. XXIX (July, 1965), 17–18.

book by Wilhelm Ernst Schmitt entitled *Steps Toward Apostasy at Wheaton College.*[35] Schmitt, a member of the Wheaton class of 1954, was attracted to the anticommunist movement after personally witnessing the student demonstrations against the House Committee on Un-American Activities hearings in San Francisco in May, 1960. He published a lengthy article defending the controversial film *Operation Abolition* which launched him on the road to fame as an expert in anticommunism. He was associated for a while with the Schwarz organization and in 1963–64 served as head of the research staff of the Church League of America. At this time he prepared and paid for the printing of a manuscript exposing the college's "trend toward the Left."

The book must rank as one of the most malicious documents to come from the pen of a professing Christian in the last decade. Schmitt reveals a total ignorance of the nature of higher education and regards a Christian college merely as an instrument of indoctrination. Since he was aware of the conservative nature of Wheaton's constituency, he embarked upon a one-man campaign to remold the college in the image of an anticommunist training institute. He seemed oblivious of the fact that his political tract could very well have resulted in the destruction or the reduction to utter insignificance of this distinguished evangelical Christian school. His venomous attacks were potentially capable of driving away Wheaton's competent faculty and discouraging donors from supporting a school that "coddles collectivists and welcomes socialists and subversives to the campus and to the faculty."

What had aroused the ire of Schmitt? For one thing,

[35] Wheaton, Ill.: Privately printed, 1966.

the statement "Wheaton is conservative in its political and economic views," found in the 1963–64 college catalog, was replaced in the subsequent edition by "Wheaton is conservative in its theological position." Speakers and entertainers were permitted on campus who in the judgment of this disgruntled alumnus possessed "serious records of pro-Communist involvements." Some professors had attacked such "responsible anti-Communist organizations and their representatives" as the John Birch Society, Church League of America, and Christian Anti-Communism Crusade, and had actually criticized campus speakers who evidenced a conservative or antisocialist outlook. Moreover, the college student body had joined the "left-wing" dominated National Student Association. (Schmitt had not at that time heard that the C.I.A. was behind it!) The student publications carried writings that "spouted the pro-socialist and Communist-propaganda line," while guest lecturers sometimes spoke favorably about the "liberal, left-wing dominated" National Council of Churches and the ecumenical movement.[36]

Schmitt's technique was the classic Radical Right smear. He singled out seven visiting lecturers (including Harry Golden, Arnold Toynbee, and missionary leader Arthur Glasser) and ten faculty members, and proceeded to list their left-wing and "communist" affiliations, drawing heavily from the data assembled in the Church League's files. Even the appearance of one's name in a *New York Times* advertisement could be incriminating, and to be mentioned unfavorably by a witness before the House Un-American Activities Committee was unequivocal evidence of guilt. Statements

[36] *Ibid.*, pp. 10–11.

made and positions taken by these individuals were
twisted to make them appear in the worst possible light.
Faculty members who participated in civil-rights activities or who sought in an intelligent manner to approach
issues relating to communism were subjected to vilification, while considerable space was devoted to discredit-
ing the actions of student leaders and the college's jour-
nalistic organs. Even top administrators V. Raymond
Edman and Hudson T. Armerding were not spared
Schmitt's free-swinging verbal assaults. His conclusion:
the college, "for 100 years a stronghold of Conservatism
and American ideals," was being penetrated by the insidious forces of modernism and collectivism and that immediate action was necessary to make the Wheaton
community aware of the terrible menace of the communist conspiracy.[87]

The Christian Far Right also dissipates the efforts of
thousands of sincere believers to propagate the Gospel.
Their time, strength, and money are diverted to the
struggle against collectivism or for free enterprise instead
of the higher calling of God. The well-known missionary
Don Hillis accurately described this situation when he
wrote: "In the lives of some, anti-communism conversa-
tion has usurped Bible study. Anti-communism movements have supplanted missions. A warm and zealous
witness which at one time gave world evangelism its
priority has in some hearts been dethroned by a neurotic
negativism which spends its energy fighting communism." [38]

One other way in which Christian Rightism under-
mines genuine Christianity is the idolatrous manner in

[87] *Ibid.,* pp. 170–73.
[38] Hillis, *op. cit.,* p. 17.

which it links the faith to political conservatism. Billy James Hargis told John Redekop that he could not see how a "born again believer" could be anything but a conservative politically. A person who is true to his "Christian calling" would identify with the Far Right.[39] John Stormer (author of *None Dare Call It Treason*[40]) states in his second book, *The Death of a Nation*,[41] that men had failed in the struggle against communism, socialism, and political liberalism because they had been fighting "in their own strength." All anticommunist programs will fail "unless they are implemented in the power of God." This secularization of the Christian faith debases it and may in the long run do more damage to Christianity than a movement which has no room for God in its philosophy.

The Far Right is truly a parasitic movement which threatens to ruin the effectiveness of orthodox Christianity. It takes advantage of the zeal and dedication of Christian believers and misuses the name of Jesus Christ for political purposes. Evangelicals must beware of the insidious attempts of Christian Rightists to exploit their religious concerns and to yoke the faith to an ultraconservatism that violates the basic ethical principles of Christianity. Those threatened by Rightist agitators should heed the injunction of James: "Resist the devil and he will flee from you" (James 4:7).

[39] Redekop, *op. cit.*, p. 189.
[40] Florissant, Mo.: Liberty Bell Press, 1964.
[41] Florissant, Mo.: Liberty Bell Press, 1968, p. 55.

III Freedom or Slavery

No one can serve two masters; for either he will hate the one and love the other, or he will be devoted to the one and despise the other. You cannot serve God and mammon. (Matthew 6:24)

Therefore because you trample upon the poor and take from him exactions of wheat, you have built houses of hewn stone, but you shall not dwell in them; you have planted pleasant vineyards, but you shall not drink their wine. For I know how many are your transgressions, and how great are your sins. (Amos 5:11–12)

An informed Christian recognizes that Communism and Christianity are completely incompatible and that there is no "half-truth" or "passion for social justice" in Communism. . . . It is an international conspiracy of gangsters. The Communist system exists for the very purpose of enforcing an evil, consciously atheistic code of behavior. . . . Communist rulers are the Devil's representatives who are engaged in total war to spread their Red Hell throughout the globe. (The Rev. Herman J. Otten, Lutheran minister) [1]

[1] Herman J. Otten, *Baal or God* (New Haven, Mo.: Leader Publishing Co. [1965]), p. 298.

God's positive will for society will not be proclaimed
when the church spends most of her energy combating
"creeping socialism," the Communist menace, or other
real or imagined enemies. Communists will never overthrow our government if we successfully control the social
problems which allow them to gain a foothold. A positive
attack on poverty, unemployment, mental illness, disease,
political corruption, racial discrimination, materialism,
hedonism, moral decadence, juvenile delinquency, the
population explosion, injustice, and other social problems
is the best way to hamper Communist propaganda. The
way to overcome evil is to do good. (David O. Moberg) [2]

Confusion and Misunderstanding About Communism

The Unequal Yoke of evangelical Christianity and
political conservatism has generated a serious understanding gap with regard to communism and how to deal
with it. Because most orthodox Christians have no comprehension of the forces that produce communism or the
attraction it has for people, they are easily led astray by
the prophets of the Far Right with their ready-made
answers and easy explanations to difficult problems.
They are easy prey for fearmongers who seek to arouse
devout believers to action in a manner such as that of
Texas evangelist William Opie: "Communism must be
crushed before it destroys all the benefits that civilization has created for mankind. Communism is mankind's
greatest enemy. We must destroy Communism before it
destroys us." [3]

[2] Moberg, *op. cit.*, p. 94.
[3] William Edward Opie, *The Cry of the Kremlin* (Dallas, Tex.:
Loftin-Shepherd, 1961), p. 58.

The difficulty arises in part out of a faulty understanding of American history. Conservatives, like all people with strong ideological commitments, tend to cherish a view of the past that reinforces their own ideas about the present. They usually feel that American history has been shaped by leaders who were devout Christians and hard-working, rugged individualists and who built this country into the most dynamic political and economic power in the world. However, in 1933 the United States reached a turning point and rapidly tumbled from its pinnacle of moral excellence. The newsletter of the group Awake America for Christ describes what happened:

> The soul of America began to be sold during the Franklin Roosevelt administrations. A price was placed on truth when this country recognized the anti-Christian regime of Red Russia. The process of deterioration and destruction of our free society under God became accelerated under the leadership of Harvard eggheads. God gave us a chance in 1942–5 to be rid of both Nazism and Communism; instead our anti-Christian leaders chose to groom Communism for world leadership.
>
> The providence of God gave us a respite under the administration of Eisenhower and Nixon, but it proved too little too late. The Kennedy administration began the final sell-out of this country to anti-Christian Communism.[4]

Of course, more responsible conservatives do not view the last forty years in such extreme terms, although they are critical of much that has transpired. Some, such as Edward Coleson, feel that Roosevelt was guilty of fallacious economic thinking (government planning and easy

[4] Quoted in Robert A. Rosenstone, *Protest from the Right* (Beverly Hills, Calif.: Glencoe Press, 1968), pp. 2–3.

money) while the United States grew soft on communism and engaged in a global giveaway.[5] In his treatment
of American history C. Gregg Singer argues that a fundamental ideological reorientation took place during this
period. Individual evil was downgraded in favor of social
sin and responsibility, and the proper approach to the
problem of evil was considered to be legislation which
would reform society "according to the thinking of those
in sociology, psychology and economics who were greatly
influenced by Marxian philosophy and who had little
regard for the American constitutional system or heritage." In World War II the liberals continued their
unceasing labors to bring about a democratically con-
trolled collectivism in this country.[6] In short, the conservative interpretation of American history holds that
the country has suffered in the twentieth century from a
serious measure of moral and ideological subversion
which left it incapable of mounting any genuinely effective resistance to the communist advance in the world.

The problem has been complicated by the rhetorical
excesses of conservative Christian spokesmen, whose
emotional attacks on communism contribute absolutely
nothing in the way of understanding. What real meaning do any of the following statements have? "Communism is a religion spawned in hell by Satan himself in his
ruthless, relentless war against Christianity." Communism "is the Devil's brain child. It looks very much like
his last trump card." "Communism is a Satanic force.
. . . A free nation, a democracy, either must oppose
Communism or be destroyed by it. We should clean out
the Communist sympathizers in our government and

[5] Edward Coleson, *The Harvest of Twenty Centuries* (Spring Arbor,
Mich.: Spring Arbor College, 1967), pp. 331–40.
[6] Singer, *op. cit.*, p. 252; cf. chaps. 7 and 8.

remove the men who are 'soft' toward Communism."
"All of Communism is based upon a lie." "Communism
is sadism personified. It is statism perfected. The lowest
instincts of human nature are propagated and expanded.
It revels in degradation, just as a hog revels in its wallow
of filthy mud." "Communism is atheism on the march.
It is a Satanic international criminal conspiracy against
civilization, based upon a God-denying philosophy of
life." "America is in danger! We have to take a stand for
Christ or Communism. God will not tolerate an 'in
between' compromise." "At an early age, each student
should be taught that the issue is clear cut—freedom
versus slavery." Everyone in the Western world and particularly the United States "who courageously and un-
equivocably opposes Red doctrine is marked for slaughter
if and when Communism takes over." [7]

The danger of an exaggerated anticommunism arising
from an inadequate comprehension of the nature of the
ideology must not be underestimated. When communism is viewed in such absolute terms, people are prone
to demand extreme measures to combat its influence and
spread, including restrictions on civil freedom. Victor
Ferkiss indicated quite pointedly that "repression of civil
liberties, even when imposed in the name of anti-communism, only strengthens the Communist cause in the

[7] William P. Strube, Jr., *The Star over the Kremlin* (Grand Rapids,
Mich.: Baker, 1962), p. 51; McIntire, "*Author of Liberty*," p. 158; Dr.
Bob Jones, Jr., quoted in Campbell, *op. cit.*, p. 95; Billy James Hargis,
Communist America . . . Must It Be? (Tulsa, Okla.: Christian Cru-
sade, 1960), p. 40; Opie, *op. cit.*, p. 55; Otten, *op. cit.*, p. 278; John
Noble, column in *United Evangelical Action*, Vol. XVIII (November,
1959), p. 11; Fred Schwarz, *You Can Trust the Communists (to Be
Communists)* (Englewood Cliffs, N.J.: Prentice-Hall, 1960), p. 178;
Murch, "The Nature of the Beast," *United Evangelical Action*, Vol.
XVI (February 1, 1958), p. 7.

Freedom or Slavery 79

long run by conditioning the public to accept without question whatever the government wants to do." [8] Such actions constitute as much, if not more, of a threat to American freedom than communism itself. Even FBI director J. Edgar Hoover warned against "the self-styled experts on communism" who were dispensing erroneous and distorted information and causing hysteria and misplaced apprehension among the American people.[9] This admonition was directed particularly at the Radical Rightists, but it is certainly applicable to a great many evangelicals today, especially those in the fundamentalist groups.

Moreover, anticommunist extremism has a most serious negative effect upon evangelical Christianity itself. The religious anticommunism crusades equate Christianity with capitalism, and communism with the Antichrist, thus tying the faith to an established social and economic system. This identification makes it extremely difficult for Christians in communist countries to bear an effective witness. Further, as Don Hillis shows, Christian anticommunism is often harmful to missionary endeavors. In many parts of Latin America, for example, Roman Catholicism and capitalism have become virtually synonymous. Because the establishment is despotic and tyrannical, fosters class distinctions, and stifles freedom of thought, communism appears to many Latins as a better alternative. If evangelicals have nothing better to offer than Christian anticommunism, then the ministry of the Gospel will be thwarted. And just because communism is atheistic, does that make it any

[8] Victor Ferkiss, *Communism Today: Belief and Practice* (Glen Rock, N.J.: Paulist Press, 1962), p. 186.
[9] J. Edgar Hoover, "Shall It Be Law or Tyranny?" *American Bar Association Journal*, Vol. XLVIII (February, 1962), p. 120.

more antichristic than polytheism, pantheism, or Islam?
What if the church devoted its time and money to
anti-Hinduism or anti-Islam crusades? Would this not
put an end to the preaching of the Gospel in many parts
of the world? [10]

It is clear that the anticommunism to which so many
evangelicals fervently adhere should be subjected to
more careful analysis. Is it all so simple? Is communism
merely a matter of freedom versus slavery?

Individualism

Two terms which conservatives use constantly are "individualism" and "collectivism." Individualism is
equated with unregulated economic activity, private
ownership and control of property (including productive
assets), and sharply limited governmental powers. Collectivism is applied to almost anything that goes beyond
this narrowly defined individualism, such as welfare statism, state-supervised economic planning, publicly
owned business enterprises, and of course socialism and
communism.

Evangelical conservatives add a further dimension to
individualism, namely, a religious one. The point is
made repeatedly in sermons, books, and articles that
Jesus emphasized the individual to the exclusion of
groups and that the free-enterprise system is divinely
ordained. James DeForest Murch once remarked that
the parables of Jesus show how highly he valued the
individual since they refer to specific people—a certain
poor widow, a certain householder, a certain rich man.
The parables were not about races, nations, or institu-

[10] Hillis, *op. cit.*, p. 18.

tions, but rather they had a personal thrust that inspired personal commitment and action.[11] Moreover, Jesus died to save individuals and faith in Christ is a personal, not corporate, matter. A resource book prepared for use by Sunday School teachers of the Church of Christ (Christian Church) insists that the basic truth in Christianity is "that Jesus is the Savior of the individual, that the church is to aid in building up individuals into the likeness of Christ, [and] that Christian civilization is a way of life that exalts, develops, and protects the individual."[12]

Every Christian individualist can marshal an assortment of proof texts to show that "Jesus recognized free enterprise as not inconsistent with His plan."[13] For example, the parable of the vineyard owner who pays all the workers the same wage conveys the message that Christ recognized the right of a man to do as he wishes with his property (Matthew 20:1–16). The story of the householder who leased his property to a group of unfaithful tenants is a further validation of the principle of private ownership (Matthew 21:33–41). The parable of the talents reveals how Jesus looked with favor upon the realm of economic activity and praised the most aggressive and successful businessmen (Matthew 25:14–30). The account of the pounds again demonstrates his approval of the profit motive (Luke 19:11–27). The Ten Commandments are mentioned in every discussion, and a host of other verses can be and often are lifted from their contexts to reinforce individualism.

[11] Murch, *Protestant Revolt,* pp. 296–97.
[12] M. M. Blair, *Christ, Christianity, and Communism* (Cincinnati: Standard, 1950 [1966]), p. 134.
[13] Verne Paul Kaub, *Collectivism Challenges Christianity* (Winona Lake, Ind.: Light and Life Press, 1946), p. 138.

These conservatives stress *laissez-faire* (unregulated) capitalism as the form of economic endeavor which is most nearly Christian. They are opposed to any form of government interference in the economy except to preserve order and protect private property. The owner of a business "has the right of management under the law of God." [14] Hence, organized labor has no right to usurp this prerogative any more than the government has. The idea that there might be a distinction between property rights and human rights is simply a communist insinuation. Property rights, instead of being something distinct from personal rights, actually are personal ones. The owner of property must have the freedom to do as he pleases with his possessions.

Competition is of vital significance in a free-enterprise capitalist system. This results in improvement of the product and the producer as well. Those who fail in one area learn from their mistakes, and because of the challenge of free enterprise they turn failure to success in some other field of endeavor, and all society profits from their experience. The view that intense competition among children may damage them is, in the eyes of one evangelical preacher, a "socialist attitude." He suggests that competition should be encouraged, not hindered. "Competition is healthy. If it were not, athletic games and sports would be breeding crime; when, in fact, the opposite is the truth." [15] Thus, competition brings out the best in the individual; he learns how to make decisions and develops a strong sense of self-reliance and independence.

This system is basically Christian, we are told, because

[14] McIntire, "*Author of Liberty*," p. 127.
[15] William Steuart McBirnie, *Teach Your Child Free Enterprise!* (Glendale, Calif.: Voice of Americanism, n.d.), p. 14.

in order to succeed a man must turn to God for direction. Since the individual cannot depend on the state or other people, he must look to the moral law for guidance and this results in the development of moral character. He is able to determine what his attitude will be toward his Creator and his fellowman. Further, such a system produces an environment in which Christianity can flourish and have a decisive impact upon the lives of men. As Christian layman Verne Kaub put it: "The free enterprise system is the best system under which to operate if we wish to preserve Christianity." [16]

But is this type of individualism such a moral boon? Certain questions immediately come to mind: First, if there are no restraints, might not a person struggle to the top totally oblivious of the moral law, trampling underfoot all who get in his way? Is freedom not likely to turn to license and despotism, especially when it is coupled with enormous power and the absence of restraining forces? Second, what concern for individual welfare is present in the creed of *laissez-faire?* Do the underprivileged individuals in society have any way of learning the meaning of freedom or does this right belong only to the privileged people? Third, what is property? Is it only material possessions? If so, Christianity has been wed to a highly crass form of materialism. But what about nonmaterial types of possessions—for instance, a person's reputation or life history? If these are his property, what right does the Church League of America have to maintain a secret file on the life histories of individuals? What business does Carl McIntire, or other anticommunist crusaders, have in publicly impugning the reputa-

[16] Kaub, *op. cit.,* pp. 125, 150; Kershner, *God, Gold and Government,* p. 137.

84 The Unequal Yoke

tions of ministers or college professors who happen to hold different political views from theirs? It appears that some conservatives have a rather selective definition of property: one that fits in beautifully with the interests of the wealthy. Could it be that these Christians are trying to serve two masters?

The thoughtful evangelical must not be deceived by the proponents of *laissez-faire* capitalism. There are good reasons for him to be critical of economic libertarianism. For one thing, the individualist ethic is all too often a contradiction of Christianity. Frequently, individualism camouflages the exploitation of the many in the interest of the few, and, as Claude Evans notes, it "becomes a device which allows a few powerful individuals and groups out of touch with the Christian ethic to manipulate society for their own individualistic and group ends." [17] The emphasis on success and materialism, the dog-eat-dog competition, the exploitation of the weak by the strong all negate the right of such a conception of individualism to claim the title "Christian." Evangelical historian Russell Bishop has aptly asked: "Why should an economic theory which places human self-love and self-interest at the very core of societal relationships be regarded as the best of all possible economic systems for the Christian?" [18]

Also, it should be underscored that from a Christian standpoint an economic system should have as its primary task the meeting of human needs. But the individualism of free-enterprise capitalism relegates this to a secondary position in favor of the economic advantages of

[17] J. Claude Evans, "Beyond Individualism and Collectivism," *Christian Century*, Vol. LXXXV (June 12, 1968), p. 778.
[18] Russell K. Bishop, "Too Much Free Trade and Adam Smith," *Fides et Historia*, Vol. I (Spring, 1969), p. 30.

those who exercise power over its institutions. About this the Christian cannot remain silent. The New Testament stands in judgment over every system which subordinates human beings to material things. The Jesus who said a man is of much more value than a sheep will not look lightly upon an economic philosophy that reduces man to a mere commodity whose value is determined solely by the impersonal forces of the market and by those who control these forces. Orthodox Protestants have always believed that no human institution or system can be given final and uncritical devotion, and this holds in the economic realm as well. To equate Christianity with economic libertarianism is to be guilty of idolatry, the violation of the Second Commandment. It behooves the sincere Christian to separate himself from such a practice at once.

Collectivism

"Collectivism" is the great bugaboo of all conservatives, whether they are Christian or not. It is difficult to ascertain what a writer or speaker means when he uses the term, as it may be applied to any kind of left-leaning political and economic system ranging from a mild welfare state to the most rigid Stalinist regime. Christian conservatives see it as stemming from a declining faith in individualism and the power of God to transform society. They argue that the Christian way is to change individuals through love and persuasion, and then they will make an impact on the world, while collectivism is social change brought about by the power of the state. Further, they suggest that the desire for a collectivist order has been intensified by mistaken but well-meaning

religious leaders who thought they were advancing the
New Testament teaching of brotherly love.

Collectivism is viewed as a harsh existence that violates human freedom and divine law. The individual is
subordinated to the group, loses his individuality, and
can no longer follow his own conscience. He must obey
the state in all things, and this takes precedence over
obedience to God. His possessions, services, and very life
are in the hands of the state and the political leaders
who control it. Instead of loving one's neighbor as himself, the person is coerced by the state on behalf of the
neighbor. Wealth is equalized by force, even though
Jesus had refused to do that himself, and such action
ignores the differences which God created in men. Even
the family loses significance, because the ideology of
collectivism "clashes with the concepts of home and
family." In the family the individual is nurtured and
respected while in a collectivist order he is under "a
wholly independent super-authority," namely, the
state.[19]

Collectivism is actually a Satanic plot. The devil had
been cast out of heaven for trying to usurp the place of
God, and now he has donned the seductive attire of
collectivism in order to try "to dethrone God and en-
slave man." He is making a new attempt to gain sovereignty "through the welfare state." His tactic is to seize
the wealth of some people in order allegedly to be kind
to all who are in need until finally he destroys their
self-reliance, gains control over them, and places them in
bondage by the power of government. Thus, through the
device of socialism, Satan seeks to transfer man's allegiance from God to the all-powerful state.[20]

[19] Kaub, *op. cit.*, pp. 118–19.
[20] Kershner, *God, Gold and Government*, pp. 42, 122, 134.

Nearly all Christian conservatives complain about the "atheism" of collectivism. A socialist system, in the words of Orthodox Presbyterian minister Francis Mahaffy, denies "the right of the Creator to set the norms of conduct in his creation" and hence is characterized by a "practical atheism." [21] It is open rebellion against God and his purpose which is the creation of individuals who have freedom to order their lives. One writer declared that if "the economy of free choice" is destroyed, "we will have gone a long way toward replacing Christian principles with the Atheism of the Collective movement. . . . Freedom and Christianity go hand in hand." [22] In a widely distributed book put out by the Free Methodist publishing house, Verne Kaub flatly stated that "if America were persuaded, or tricked into abandonment of free enterprise in favor of any form of collectivism . . . Christianity as we know it, openly professed, practiced, and taught, would end." Further, he maintained that "every collectivist state, by whatever name, must be anti-Christian." [23] In sum, these conservatives are saying that personal liberty originates from God, and that if a people compromises this freedom in any manner by surrendering a portion of it to the state, even though this may be intended only to enlarge the scope of freedom for all individuals, they deny God's right to direct their lives and become for all practical purposes atheistic. For many evangelicals today, collectivism is the secular counterpart of atheism.

Collectivism, whether manifested in the form of government involvement in social welfare or in a more

---

[21] Francis E. Mahaffy, "The Fruit of Communism: Socialistic Redistribution," *The Freeman*, Vol. XVII (September, 1967), p. 570.

[22] *The Brian Bex Report* (no date), excerpted in *Schism*, Vol. I (Summer, 1969), p. 31.

[23] Kaub, *op. cit.*, pp. 12, 108.

highly developed socialist order, leads—we are assured
—inexorably to communism. Schemes such as urban
renewal, public housing, Medicare, and Social Security
are part of a gigantic conspiracy to undermine the free
institutions of the United States. Because the collectivist
movement is materialistic and basically Marxian, it aims
at the eventual establishment of a full-blown communist
order; hence Christians should resist all "socialist tendencies." This viewpoint has been expressed with varying
degrees of intensity by evangelical leaders. A few examples will suffice. Harold John Ockenga was quoted in the
N.A.E. organ as saying that socialistic schemes "soften
society for Marxism," while Albert J. Lindsey told an
N.A.E. convention in Chicago that socialism is "nothing
more than a prep school for communism." [24] James De-
Forest Murch insisted "the Social Gospel is little more
or less than Socialism. . . . It is only a step from this to
Communism." [25] The editor of the Evangelical Sunday
School Lesson Commentary contended that because the
Communists knew "the Church and the Sunday School
have had a persuasive influence on the warp and woof
of our successful free enterprise system," they "set about
to synthesize socialistic dogma with Christian doctrine." [26]

The Christian conservatives who are disturbed about
the advance of government intervention in economic
and social affairs have overlooked the fact that this is not
a novelty. The very nature of government requires such

[24] *United Evangelical Action*, Vol. XVII (March 15, 1958), p. 6;
(July 15, 1958), p. 4.
[25] Murch, *Protestant Revolt*, p. 38.
[26] Wilbur G. Williams, "Socialist Penetration of Religious Education Material," in Kenneth Ingwalson, ed., *Your Church—Their
Target* (Arlington, Va.: Better Books, 1966), pp. 151–52.

action, as the phrase in the preamble to the Constitution "promote the general welfare" so clearly indicates. A democratic government is concerned about the welfare of individual persons—not *some* individuals but *all* of them. The increasing complexities of modern society and the interdependence of all mankind make it mandatory that the government play a larger role in meeting social problems. The day of rugged individualism is past; the world is too crowded and too complex. Private solutions to such perplexing problems as industrialization, urbanization, pollution, racial discrimination, and poverty fall woefully short of alleviating the human suffering caused by them. As David Moberg has so ably pointed out: "The welfare of all is linked with the welfare of others; to promote the general welfare, government must promote the welfare of all segments of the population." [27]

It is wrong to assume that "socialism" and "communism" are necessarily one and the same thing, in spite of the confusion and vagueness that surround these terms. Democratic socialism puts its primary emphasis on the individual human being and enhancing the quality of his life, and does not see him as the object of impersonal forces or the absolute state as communism does. To be sure, socialism may absolutize the collective in the same manner that individualism absolutizes itself. The collectivist may forget God and concentrate solely upon the quest for community and security. In point of fact, individualism and collectivism need each other. Individualism stresses freedom and responsibility to God while collectivism emphasizes security and obligations to one's fellowman. A system that professes to be Christian

[27] Moberg, *op. cit.*, p. 129.

should include elements of both, not forgetting, of
course, that the Gospel must exercise judgment over it in
the same manner as it does over all systems.

What Is Communism?

The hang-up on individualism versus collectivism, together with the legacy of Cold War rhetoric and stereo-
types about communism, explain in large measure why
until recently most of the literature by evangelical Christians dealing with the topic ranked scarcely above the
level of propaganda.[28] Political scientist Will Adams has
revealed just how muddleheaded much of the Christian
thinking about communism is. By wrenching statements
by communists from context, critics succeed in proving
whatever they wish about the ideology. These spokesmen credit communists with everything that they claim
to have accomplished on the world scene and often
much more, and they make comparisons between the
Soviet and American systems that fail to distinguish
ideals from realities. Utilizing the devil theory of politics, such commentators show that every communist
move is part of a gigantic conspiracy by dehumanized
supermen capable of limitless evil and superhuman
achievements to bring about the destruction of freedom.

[28] The striking exceptions to this are two books by Lester DeKoster
of Calvin College, *Communism and the Christian Faith*, rev. ed.
(Grand Rapids, Mich.: Eerdmans, 1962), and *Vocabulary of Communism* (Grand Rapids, Mich.: Eerdmans, 1964). Also worthy of note
are two works by a Southern Baptist and a Methodist seminary professor, Henlee H. Barnette, *An Introduction to Communism* (Grand
Rapids, Mich.: Baker, 1964), and Carl O. Bangs, *The Communist
Encounter: Vital Christianity Is the Only Answer* (Kansas City, Mo.:
Beacon Hill Press, 1963).

Further, they stress the monolithic nature of communism, totally disregarding the realities of the Sino-Soviet split, and emphasize the absolute primacy of ideological considerations in dictating every Russian action. In short, communism is portrayed as the root of all trouble in the world regardless of local social and economic conditions, the existence of long-standing international quarrels, or the desires of ambitious politicians to gain power.[29]

That such an understanding of communism is held by many evangelicals is indeed unfortunate. Therefore, it would be well at this point to say a few words about the origins of the ideology and some of its distinguishing points. The basic doctrines of communism were spelled out by a nineteenth-century German intellectual, Karl Marx, and his close friend, Friedrich Engels, who were trying to deal with the problems of the working class in modern industrial society. Marxist thought had some influence on the development of the European labor movement but accomplished little until the doctrines were molded into an action program by the Russian V. I. Lenin. He organized a revolutionary party that in 1917 seized the reins of power in his land and began reconstructing the state along the lines of the communist ideology. After Lenin's death his successor, J. V. Stalin, relented on efforts to export the doctrine and concentrated on internal developments in Russia, now renamed the Soviet Union. After World War II the victorious Soviet armies aided in installing communist regimes in Eastern Europe, thereby creating a satellite empire. At the same time the influence of communist ideas in the

[29] William W. Adams, Jr., "Communism, Realism, and Christianity," in *Protest and Politics*, pp. 205–17.

non-Western world steadily increased, and communist regimes came into power in North Korea, China, North Vietnam, and finally Cuba. As Marxist-Leninist parties grew in importance throughout the world, the Western powers became increasingly apprehensive about the spread of communism, particularly in the late 1940's and the 1950's (the Cold War years). The question of relations with communist governments and halting the spread of the ideology has been the primary concern of American policy for the past quarter century.

One characteristic of communism is the materialist conception of history, that is, the conviction that the production and exchange of goods and services supporting human life offer the fundamental explanation for all social processes and institutions. This economic factor is the most important one in history and is the foundation on which the superstructure of human society—its laws, government, culture, social relationships and their corresponding political, social, religious, and artistic ideologies—is erected. Those who control the fundamental economic processes dictate the type of social and political institutions which will develop in the society. Ideas and religious teachings are nothing more than reflections of the basic economic interests in society.

Change takes place when the forces of production expand and thereby alter the economic foundation of society. Thus, an agriculturally based society changes into one based on commerce, or the commercially based one is changed into an industrial society. However, social change lags behind, so that in a commercial society many of the institutions of the older feudal society are still present. Those people who are intimately involved with the new mode of production are forced to challenge those presently in control of the political and social structures, because these outmoded structures hinder the full expansion of the productive forces in society. Thus, class struggle is a vital element in the historical process.

In the industrial society the working class (proletariat) is now the largest group and the one most closely related to the forces of production. However, the capitalist class (bourgeoisie), now the outmoded one, stands in the way of progress. Because of their control over the institutions of society, the capitalists refuse to allow change that would permit full utilization of technological resources. The private ownership of property and production for profit actually hold back the productive forces in society, and so a new system of productive relations based on production for use, not profit, and common, not private, ownership of productive assets is needed. When this social system is implemented, man's capacity to turn out the vital goods needed for existence will find its fullest expression.

This lag between technological know-how and the existing social and political institutions can be overcome only by revolution. The ruling class will use the legal, political, and ideological instruments of the society to block the growth of the forces which arise from the new, more progressive economic system. A social and political system does not freely surrender power to its successor, but rather power must be seized. Hence, the transformation from capitalism to communism will be made by force and will take place only after a long period of struggle in which the ruling class clings desperately to power. Nevertheless, the victory of the proletariat is inevitable. After they have won, they will proceed through dictatorial methods to dismantle the superstructure of the capitalist order and usher in the communist millennium, the so-called classless society.

Revolution is a key doctrine, especially as it is developed by Lenin. Marx believed that the working class would spontaneously develop a sense of class consciousness, leaders would emerge from their ranks who would take charge of the struggle for power, and finally the proletariat would win out by the sheer weight of its numbers. Lenin however stressed the importance of the professional revolutionary in the struggle for power. The professionals were to be tightly organized and would work conspiratorially to overthrow the existing order. The party is all-important because it would plan and execute the revolution.

Ethics in the communist doctrine is dependent on the interests of the class struggle. Ethical systems are merely the reflection of the economic base of society, and thus there are no absolutes, no eternal truths. Any means that promotes the end of the struggle for power is justified, be it compromise, lying, murder, war, etc. The idea of a divine ethical standard is rejected out of hand. Religion is just as much an outgrowth of the forces of production as any other social, legal, political, or artistic form. Thus, Christianity is only a device of the ruling class which it uses to hold back the tide of revolution, and in the classless society there will be no need for God.

Yet, it is interesting that communism as it is practiced today manifests most of the characteristics of a religion. Although it rejects the idea of a supreme being and the immortality of the soul, it is still very much a rival faith to Christianity. Ralph Moellering has pointed out a number of areas where the ideology has religious overtones. First, communism maintains that there is ultimate purpose in history, and in the movement toward the final goal of perfection man plays an important role. The concept of God in the process is replaced by that of

dialectical conflict between those who control the forces
of production and those who are in charge of the social
and political institutions. Also, there is a trinity in communism. The creative power (clash and conflict) is
imbedded in the dialectic (God the Father). This erupts
in revolution and thus a messianic figure (Marx or
Lenin) appears. The Communist Party (the Holy
Spirit) directs the actions of the believers. Moreover,
there are saints, those far-sighted men who grasped the
real significance of the economic and social changes of
their times and who prescribed solutions to the political
and economic problems. Included are such people as
Marx, Engels, Lenin, and other figures who may be
canonized from time to time. There are icons (pictures
and statues of the great men), relics (to be displayed and
admired), and rites at their shrines (Lenin's tomb).
There is a body of sacred scriptures, the writings of
Marx, Engels, Lenin, Mao Tse-tung, and other prophets
of communism.

Like all religions there are criteria for maintenance of
orthodoxy. Heretics are expelled and denounced, or even
subjected to punishment by excommunication, imprison-
ment, or execution. Deviants include Trotskyites, Tito-
ists, bourgeois socialists, and various mavericks who are
singled out from time to time. There are group-worship
services, such as great rallies in theaters and public
squares, complete with sermons and exhortations by
leaders and antiphonal cheers from the crowds. The
convert to communism must repudiate his past connec-
tions and repent of his affiliation with capitalism or any
other reactionary doctrine. He must surrender his entire
life to the communist cause, and even undergo such
things as ideological indoctrination (catechism?) and
regular confession in local cell groups. Communism also

has a missionary vision. Like evangelists, communists work among the people to spread the ideology and the gospel of revolution which will bring about peace and prosperity for all mankind, not just the privileged classes. There is a millennial view, the classless society where all men will be free and happy, where exploitation will be no more. Finally, the communist believes that victory is inevitable. Just as the Christian looks toward the final triumph of Christ over sin, so the communist looks forward to the ultimate downfall of capitalism.[80] Thus, the Marxist-Leninist doctrine has all the qualities of a secular religion; it can fill the void in the hearts of men who have given up their traditional beliefs, much like the record of the unclean spirit which had left a man but came back to him with seven other spirits more evil than himself so that his last state became worse than his first (Matthew 12:43–45).

Why Is Communism Attractive?

As much as conservative Christians dislike communism, it is impossible to deny that it does appeal to many people. One lure it has is anticolonialism. The Soviet Union always verbally endorses the desires of African and Asian peoples for independent nationhood and regularly demands the immediate and unconditional abolition of colonialism. It is ironic that the Christian Gospel and missionary effort instigated many of the social changes in these lands and enabled people to obtain the education that made them aware of their position in the

[80] Ralph L. Moellering, "Communism and Christianity—An Ideological Comparison," *Concordia Theological Monthly*, Vol. XXXIV (November, 1963), pp. 645–54.

world. One would expect anticolonialism to have been a
natural outgrowth of Christianity, when in fact the opposite was true. Because Christians in the West aligned
themselves with the forces of colonialism, many non-
Western leaders turned to communism as a vehicle of
protest against the system which kept them in bondage.
Their involvement with communism, then, is purely op-
portunistic and has little to do with ideology. When
attempts are made to suppress popular movements of
this nature, people are often driven farther to the left,
such as in Cuba or Vietnam, while a hands-off approach
may result in a stunning defeat for the communists (*e.g.*,
Indonesia).

The hostility of communism to capitalism is looked
upon with favor by many. There are flaws in the system,
especially as it has developed in the United States, and
the highly individualistic free-enterprise economy is dis-
tasteful since it seems to be selfish and cruel. In backward areas an unregulated capitalistic system produces a
greater disparity between rich and poor, a problem that
has been significantly reduced in the West because of
the controls placed upon it. Western capitalists are smug
and complacent about the system and its ability to keep
up production levels, but selfishly oblivious to its social
costs.

Communism is particularly appealing to the poor of
the world as a possible means of escape from their
wretched condition. The charge that communism is materialistic, coming from a people who have the highest
living standard in the world, must fall bitterly on the
ears of those starving multitudes for whom the materialism of communism is a possible form of deliverance.
Worse still is the fact that many of those who piously
condemn the materialism of communism are found

among the ranks of America's most prosperous citizens. The remarks of Southern Baptist leader Ross Coggins should be taken to heart by every concerned Christian:

> Men who are created in the image of God will not forever endure bread-crust existence, unrelieved health problems, and educational deprivation. They will follow whatever political movement holds forth even a tenuous hope of deliverance from their precarious position. Nevermore will the masses accept poverty as the natural course of events.[31]

Communism also has an idealistic attraction. Its character of secular religion appeals to many who are of a humanitarian bent, especially the middle-class intellectual who possesses a sensitized social conscience. He can work to fight poverty and thwart the capitalist exploitation of the downtrodden, or he can join a crusade on behalf of world peace. As a religion, communism brings out the best qualities in man—courage, self-denial, discipline—and it gives him something for which to live and die. Naturally, the idealist who adheres to communism can shut out its unpleasant features in much the same manner as the Christian does with his religion.

The sense of community is an appealing feature of communism. It enables the individual to find self-realization apart from self-seeking in group action and in service to others. Communism appears as a cooperative effort to make a better world for all people, not just those who get ahead. The individual experiences fulfillment and comradeship as he works together with others of like mind in a noble cause. As an isolated individual he is

[31] Ross Coggins, *To Change the World* (Nashville, Tenn.: Broadman, 1964), p. 16.

nothing, but identification with a group that is doing something and going somewhere gives him a sense of meaning.

Finally, Soviet achievements have made a profound impression on many, especially on those in developing nations. Russia herself was a backward, war-devastated, poverty-stricken agricultural country when the communists came to power only half a century ago. Then, on the basis of their own human and material resources and under the direction of a communist regime, the Russians were able to make tremendous advances in industrialization before being ravaged once again in World War II. Yet, the Soviet Union bounced back and now is the second-ranked industrial power in the world. In some areas of science and technology Russia is now the leader, and of course there are the Soviet space exploits which have won the admiration of many in the non-Western world.

Communism then has definite positive achievements to its credit. The communist critique of bourgeois society has challenged people in the West to reassess their purpose and to build a more equitable social and political order. Marxists point out some genuine weaknesses in capitalism, such as the concentration of wealth in the hands of too few people and the tendency toward periodic cycles of prosperity and depression. Growth of trade unionism, passage of regulatory legislation, and an awakening of social consciousness among the business leaders has been the response, so that capitalism has been significantly modified and humanized. The communist vision of a better world is a clear reminder to Christians that they must redouble their efforts to achieve social justice for all men. And of course, there are the practical accomplishments in countries like the Soviet Union—increased living standards, mass public education, better medical care, advancements in science and technology, etc.[32]

On the other hand, there are some extremely serious defects in communism which make it ideologically unacceptable to Christians. First, its so-called atheism is in reality naturalism carried to its logical end. Communism denies or ignores the existence of the supernatural and focuses all attention on man alone, rather than man in relation to God. There is no idea of accountability to a Higher Being, no divine law, no future judgment. The concerns of communism are purely materialistic, meaning that there is in fact no higher goal in life than an increased production of goods and services and a more comfortable standard of living.

A second deficiency in communism is its lack of concern for human beings as individuals. Abstractions such as the party, class struggle, dialectic, and revolution assume primacy over the needs of individuals. People gain significance only in the mass. The Christian idea of each individual person having eternal significance before God is totally rejected for the temporal and material salvation of the collective social organism. When individuals stand in the way of the group, *i.e.*, the party or the state, they are pushed aside and perhaps liquidated. The isolated person in a communist system has no Bill of Rights to which he can appeal but rather is always at the mercy of the collective and its leadership.

A third shortcoming of communism is its rejection of the reality of sin. The idea that man is a sinner and in need of salvation is fundamental to Christianity. Communism, however, teaches that sin is not a violation of

[32] This matter is discussed in considerable detail in Gabriel A. Almond, *The Appeals of Communism* (Princeton, N.J.: Princeton University Press, 1954).

God's law because God does not exist. There is no need for a savior because the world can be saved without Christ. Since communists are following the laws of history, no action can be termed immoral or sinful. What aids in the destruction of the old bourgeois, capitalist world and the creation of the new socialist order is moral and ethical. The end gives ethical value to whatever means are utilized to accomplish it. Therefore, the exploiting classes and all who stand in the way of the proletarian movement can be justifiably eliminated in the interests of the class struggle. Nothing could be more diametrically opposed to the ethical standard of Jesus Christ!

What Can Christians Do About Communism? .

The foregoing discussion suggests that communism is attractive for many people and that its adherents are generally sincere in their beliefs. Yet clearly, it cannot have any true appeal for Christians. For them, the basic question must be, How can the spread of communism be checked? A purely negative approach is certainly not the answer, for this does not get at the heart of the issue. J. Edgar Hoover cautioned his fellow Americans about those individuals who "are merely against Communism without being for any positive measure to eliminate the social, political or economic frictions which the Communists are so adroit at exploiting." [33] In the same vein Methodist theologian A. Roy Eckardt declared that "time expended in verbal denunciations of the Communists would be spent more profitably in fostering deeds

[33] Hoover, "The Communist Party Line," Senate Document No. 59, 87th Cong., 1st Sess., 1961, p. 6.

of mercy, responsible and imaginative leadership, and creative counsel to this time of troubles." [34]

A good example of where unthinking anticommunism can lead is former N.A.E. Executive Secretary George L. Ford's description of an imaginary communist takeover of America and its impact on the country. Legitimate law enforcement agencies would be replaced with hoodlums and released prisoners. A gradual tightening of control over church life would take place until all churches came under complete communist domination and ministered only by permission of and in line with communist directives. Specific classes would be liquidated, particularly those concerned with the religious life of the nation and the governmental agencies. A slave-labor system would be introduced to control political enemies and produce for the communists at minimum cost. Those not liquidated or enslaved would spend their lives in the "big cage" where they would conform to the communist masters and be remade in their image. With an air of authority, Ford declares: "To expect anything different from this is to ignore the pure facts of the history of Communism." [35] What possible value do such remarks have?

Further, the negative approach of Christian anticommunism drags the children of God down to the level of the Marxists. By labeling communists as the godless tools of Satan, one evades the injunction to love all men. In order to prevent the devil from gaining any more earthly power, it is declared that these servants of his must be dealt with harshly and the Christian must use

[34] A. Roy Eckardt, *The Surge of Piety in America* (New York: Association, 1958), p. 123.

[35] George L. Ford, *The Miracle of America* (Grand Rapids, Mich.: Zondervan, 1963), p. 48.

whatever means necessary to gain the victory over the forces of evil. What is not mentioned, however, is that those leading (or giving financial support to) the Christian anticommunist struggle are all too often those who have the most to lose in the event of a communist victory, namely, representatives of the privileged classes who control the political and economic life of the United States. Clair Davis, writing in *Christianity Today*, warns evangelicals that it is "wrong to make united *opposition* to a particular movement a quasi-religion in its turn. Thus Christianity is not to be equated with, and is certainly not to be consumed by, either 'socialism' or 'anti-Communism.' " [36] The dedicated believer should have no part of the idolatrous practice of making the Christian faith an adjunct of the political struggle against communism.

There are, however, a number of positive things the Christian can do. Most important of these is the taking of one's faith seriously. As Foy Valentine suggests, "the best defense against communism is the good offense of a sound and vigorous faith in Jesus Christ." [37] This trust must be translated into a language of words and deeds as the believer seeks to bring the Gospel to bear on the problems of the world. Christianity must develop a moral and spiritual thrust which will demonstrate to the world that it offers a way of life superior to the materialism of communism. Whether this will be accomplished depends completely on the degree of commitment on the part of every Christian.

But the evangelical cannot simply stop here. He must

[36] Clair Davis, "Using the State for Sectarian Ends," *Christianity Today*, Vol. XI (June 23, 1967), p. 10.

[37] Foy Valentine, *The Cross in the Marketplace* (Waco, Texas: Word, 1966), p. 70.

be alert to the social and economic conditions which
breed communism and work to alleviate them. Everywhere Christians should be in the forefront of the struggle against poverty, disease, starvation, ignorance, overpopulation, and racial discrimination. They must not be
seduced by the false prophets of anticommunism who
play down this burning need for social justice throughout the world and stress instead the use of military force
to check the communist advance abroad and the abridg-
ment of civil liberties to eliminate alleged subversion at
home. What could be more tragic than the remark
which a young black man in South Africa made to Ross
Coggins: "When I struggle for the same rights you
Americans take for granted—freedom to come and go,
freedom of speech, freedom of the press, freedom of
worship—I am called a Communist." [38] If evangelical
Christians line up on the side of the *status quo* and
support the economic and political goals of the rich,
then the communists will win the battle for men's minds
by Christian default.

Another required task for the concerned Christian is
to become as well-informed as possible about communism. "My people are destroyed for lack of knowledge"
is the trenchant warning of the prophet Hosea (4:6).
One should become familiar with the ideology and tactics of communism by studying the basic documents and
the many competent scholarly works on Marxism-Lenin-
ism. Moreover, the Christian should be equally well
instructed in the tenets of his own faith so that he will
be aware of the basic differences between the two doctrines and be able to expose and oppose the fallacies of
communism in the light of the Gospel.

[38] Coggins, *op. cit.*, pp. 13–14.

American Christians should support endeavors to humanize communist regimes and to improve living standards in their lands. They ought not to feel that it is immoral to aid and use communists against one another. The Far Right has done the country a real disservice with its moralistic sloganeering about negotiations with communists and diplomatic and economic relations with their governments. Christians should welcome improvements in the quality of human existence in communist countries through economic aid and trade agreements, even if such advances are slow in coming.

The Christian Gospel is really the most meaningful answer to the problem of communism. Genuine freedom is to be found in Jesus Christ, not in economic individualism or any form of collectivism. In Christ one has nothing to fear, for God has given his children "a spirit of power and love" (II Timothy 1:7) and "where the Spirit of the Lord is, there is freedom" (II Corinthians 3:17). With the strength he receives through faith in Christ, the evangelical Christian should "outthink, outlive, outdo, and outdie the communists." Foy Valentine's words ring out: "Let us change the world!" [39]

[39] Valentine, *Cross in the Marketplace*, p. 74.

IV Christian Americanism . . . Must It Be?

If my people who are called by my name humble themselves, and pray and seek my face, and turn from their wicked ways, then I will hear from heaven, and will forgive their sin and heal their land. (II Chronicles 7:14)

Truly I perceive that God shows no partiality, but in every nation any one who fears him and does what is right is acceptable to him. (Acts 10:34-35)

The source of our nation's strength from its beginning has been faith in God. . . . Statesmen, leaders and outstanding citizens have indicated their faith in God through their public and private statements. The nation laid its foundation and developed its political and social structure by its continued adherence to these spiritual and religious ideals. . . . Schools, colleges, charitable institutions, hospitals, orphanages, and other institutions, are monumental proof of the Christian character of the United States of America. The true source of our nation's character has been obscured at times by current ideologies and new social theories. . . . Godliness, loyalty, and patriotism are no longer evaluated as sterling values. A new dedication to

106

the great Christian truths and beliefs which spurred our people to build a great nation in a few centuries is needed. (Benjamin Weiss, noted evangelical layman) [1]

It would be better to shuck off all pretense that the United States is a Christian nation. We should call it "a pagan nation, inhabited by a minority of committed Christians." . . . To condemn the nation, in effect, in order that some may be saved from the general wreckage, is no easy choice. Even a great evangelist like Billy Graham, whose calling is to summon men from complacent self-satisfaction to make an honest decision before God, cannot face the choice; at his crusades the old and ambiguous image of Christian America is constantly reevoked. (Harold O. J. Brown) [2]

The Image of Christian America

One of the most widely held and often proclaimed views among American evangelicals is the idea that this country is a Christian nation. Of course, invoking God's approval on the deeds and misdeeds of the state has been practiced by political leaders since time immemorial, but only in the United States has this become such a full-blown ideology. No other democratic nation has developed a doctrine quite comparable to the notions of Americanism and un-Americanism. For example, who would ever conceive of an automobile in Toronto carrying a bumper sticker which read, "The only ism for me is Canadianism," or of a student protest in Paris against

[1] Benjamin Weiss, *God in American History* (Grand Rapids, Mich.: Zondervan: 1966), p. 7.

[2] Harold O. J. Brown, *The Protest of a Troubled Protestant* (New Rochelle, N.Y.: Arlington House, 1969), pp. 72–73.

hearings of the Un-French Activities Committee? The
key role which Christianity plays in the ideology of
Americanism raises some disturbing questions and must
be examined in order to ascertain whether the integrity
of the faith has been compromised.

The affirmations of Christian Americanism have been
made in various ways by evangelical spokesmen. Dr. Bob
Jones III told a reporter: "We hold with old-fashioned
Christian Americanism. We think it made this country
great, we think it serves freedom, and we think it serves
God." [3] In his widely circulated book *Communist America . . . Must It Be?* [4] Billy James Hargis declared:
"Patriotism and Christianity are very close to each other.
It is impossible to be a true Christian and not be a true
patriot. One who loves God also loves his country. Our
forefathers believed in Jesus Christ and His atoning
blood. . . . America is and always has been a Christian
nation." But it should not be assumed that only the
right-wingers feel this way. In an *Hour of Decision* radio
sermon Billy Graham asserted that if America is going to
survive, "we are going to have to renew that faith in the
God of our fathers. . . . The secret of America's
strength has been her faith in God." [5] In the same vein,
Dr. Edward L. R. Elson, minister of the National Presbyterian Church in Washington and chaplain to the
United States Senate, informed his congregation that
"we cannot understand American history except as a
spiritual movement. The eternal God is the source of
this nation . . . and his Spirit the guide of its development. . . . When true to her genius she has a spiritual

[3] Quoted in Larry L. King, "Bob Jones University: The Buckle on
the Bible Belt," *Harper's*, Vol. CCXXXII (June, 1966), p. 58.

[4] Tulsa, Okla.: Christian Crusade, 1960, p. 35.

[5] Graham, *Changing the Tide of History* (Minneapolis: BGEA,
1966), p. 3. (An *Hour of Decision* radio sermon.)

destiny—a sense of mission derived from faith in the sovereign God." [6]

When an evangelical speaks of a Christian America, what does he mean? What image exists in his mind? It is an America which began with the founding fathers who "covenanted with God" to accept his purpose and do his will.[7] They based their society upon faith in God and his holy word, and they set out to build a unique nation in the wilderness of the New World. Free Methodist educator Paul Adams suggests that "the American forefathers, like the early Christians, were men whose vision and faith were such that they intended to turn the world upside down—and did so." [8] Guided by God, the Americans threw off the yoke of British tyranny and created a state founded on the "Author of Liberty." These Christian statesmen, endowed with divine insight, wrote a Constitution which protected their liberties in a manner that no other document had done before because it created a government of law rather than men. This law was the moral law given to mankind in the Ten Commandments and confirmed and added to by New Testament teachings. Thus, the cornerstone of this nation was the Bible and its authority, and the government built upon it was one limited in its responsibilities and strictly dependent on the people whom it served. The founding fathers continually expressed their deep faith in God, as one can see by examining the important documents of the period, the Declaration of Independence, the Constitution, the inaugural addresses of President Washington, the state constitutions, and many others.

[6] Edward L. R. Elson, "The Source of Our Life," *Decision*, Vol. X (July, 1969), p. 3.

[7] *Ibid.*

[8] Paul L. Adams, "The Moral Promise and the Decline of the American Heritage," *The Freeman*, Vol. XVIII (March, 1968), p. 178.

During the nineteenth century America grew and flour-
ished on the ethical principles of Christianity, more specifically, the Protestant form of it. This ethic was based
on a universal belief in the sovereignty of God, the
revealed law of God, the God-given freedom of the individual, and the benevolent direction of divine providence. Because of vast areas of opportunity in America,
with God's help any worthy ambition lay within the
range of achievement, and nothing could hold a person
back who had the desire to succeed. In every aspect of
life God was taken into account, while people esteemed
such Christian traits as hard work, honor, integrity, and
thrift. Merit was the best qualification for advancement,
and those who climbed the ladder of success were respected. Most of the people who stood out in political,
economic, and cultural life were God-fearing men who
based their lives on this ethic. A great majority of the
Presidents were church members, and even those who
were not acknowledged their dependence on God and
sought divine guidance during their administrations.

As the United States neared the pinnacle of economic
and political achievement, at the same time she began
turning away from God. Vast hordes of immigrants
poured into this fair land who knew not the "God of our
fathers" and who brought with them the vices of the Old
World—sloth, drunkenness, ignorance—along with alien
religions like Roman Catholicism and Judaism. With
the growth of big business, big government, and big
labor, the individual was submerged, and people came
only to think of security and material wealth. The public
schools turned away from the God-centered ideals of the
founding fathers to the secular philosophies of naturalism and scientism, and through the pernicious influence
of progressive education they became concerned merely

with the adjustment of the pupil to the changing order and the mores of a pluralistic society. The idea of fixed, absolute standards for moral conduct was thrown out.[9]

However, God did not sit idly by while his people turned away from the path of national righteousness. Even as the land was experiencing unparalleled prosperity, he sent judgment—World War I, the Great Depression, World War II. Yet, America refused to humble herself and turn from her wicked ways, and continued to live off the past accumulation of spiritual and moral strength. Since World War II, the country has slipped into rapid decline. Like an epidemic the ideology of godless communism has spread through the world, and even in America native Reds burrow away like termites at the spiritual foundations of the society. The Supreme Court acts as the protector of the communists, while at the same time it chips away at the free institutions of Christian America. Atheists continue to mount a systematic campaign to remove every mention of God from the schools and public life. Old-fashioned patriotism is downgraded and turned into a mockery. The youth have given themselves over to sex and drugs, while crime rages unchecked in the streets. The world prestige of the country has now reached an all-time low as she is mired in the Vietnam conflict which her leaders are determined not to win.

America is a Christian nation, and the symbolic evidences of her faith are to be found everywhere—the motto "In God We Trust," the national anthem and patriotic songs, the phrase "under God" in the pledge of allegiance, the practice of declaring national days of

[9] This view is summarized in Murch, *Teach or Perish!* (Grand Rapids, Mich.: Eerdmans, 1961), pp. 19–22.

prayer and thanksgiving, the inscriptions of biblical pas-
sages and references to God on the public buildings of
the land, the mention made of God in each of the fifty
state constitutions, and the innumerable references to
God in the public utterances of the country's leaders.[10]
Nonetheless, she has strayed away from the faith of her
fathers and now stands poised on the brink of national
calamity. In this frightful situation the only hope for the
United States is repentance. If she does not turn to Jesus
Christ, God will destroy her. As Billy Graham told his
radio audience: "Unless America at this tragic hour is
willing to turn to Jesus Christ and be cleansed by the
blood of Christ and know the regenerating power of the
Holy Spirit, Christ will never save this nation. When
you make your decision for Jesus Christ, it is America
making her decision through you." [11] The minister of the
Church of Reflections at famous Knott's Berry Farm in
California was even more forthright in his call for a
national revival:

> The hour has come! We must call upon every American
> patriot, every Christian, every religious man, even those
> who need religion, to join hands across this great land of
> ours. This is an urgent call—our nation is in deep trouble.
> An American Revival is needed, but we have faced trouble
> before, and each time, with God's help, we have gathered
> together the forces necessary to defeat our enemies,
> whether they be enemies from without or enemies from
> within our own borders.[12]

[10] This is described in detail in Weiss, *op. cit.*

[11] Graham, *Rioting or Righteousness* (Minneapolis: BGEA, 1967),
p. 11. (An *Hour of Decision* radio sermon.)

[12] Robert F. Williams, "Needed—An American Revival," *Christian
Economics*, Vol. XXI (October 28, 1969), p. 4.

Americans have thus infused their nationalism and patriotism with moral righteousness, producing the ideology of Americanism. Americanism goes beyond a patriot's usual devotion and loyalty to his native land and its institutions. The actions of the United States (including her foreign policy) become morally justifiable because the nation is a unique society based upon humanitarian principles aiming at enlarging the scope of liberty for all individuals. According to Robert Welch, Americanism "leads toward a society in which brotherhood and kindliness and tolerance and honesty and self-reliance and the integrity of the human personality are considered virtues." [13] Since the moral foundation of American society is the law of God, the existence of a religious dimension to the ideology of Americanism is inescapable. As President Eisenhower said at the 1955 American Legion "Back to God" observance: "Recognition of a Supreme Being is the most basic expression of Americanism. . . . Without God, there could be no American form of government, nor an American way of life." [14] The editor of *Christianity Today* finds it perfectly consistent with his position as a Christian and a patriotic American to write: "Christians ought to be the best citizens and the finest patriots. Certainly they have a prior allegiance to God Almighty. But this can only make them better Americans." [15] The essence of the country's national faith can be summed-up in the oftheard phrase "America is great because she is good."

[13] Robert Welch, *The Blue Book of the John Birch Society* (Belmont, Mass.: John Birch Society, 1961), p. 141.
[14] *The New York Times*, February 21, 1955, p. 24.
[15] "Is Patriotism Dead?" *Christianity Today*, Vol. XIII (July 4, 1969), p. 908.

Is America Really Christian?

Most serious students of American history would agree that the preceding description is a gross distortion of what has actually transpired. The reality is that the United States was not founded as a Christian nation, and hardly as a Protestant nation. The founding fathers worked from a set of assumptions derived from the eighteenth-century Enlightenment which were superimposed on the Christian assumptions which they had inherited. It is clear that they had no desire to form a secular, anti-Christian state, but neither did they wish to establish a particular variety of Christianity. The American creed of the founding fathers, as described by Sidney Mead, was one that leading Protestants of the time looked upon as "infidelity"—not so much because of what it said as for what it left unsaid (sin, the need for redemption through Christ's atoning death, the inability of man to save himself through civil righteousness, etc., were totally foreign to this creed). What exactly did the founding fathers maintain? They held that all men are equal in their claim to justice, and that governments exist to give that justice, and their authority for that reason is just. The Creator is the ultimate authority from whom these equal rights are derived. Newcomers were accepted into America upon profession of faith in the American democratic way of life and belief in America's creed. This is not Christianity in the true sense, but rather rationalism, deism, or natural religion.[16]

The principle which the founding fathers accepted

[16] Sidney E. Mead, "The Post-Protestant Concept and America's Two Religions," *Religion in Life*, Vol. XXXIII (Spring, 1964), pp. 196–99.

was that of religious pluralism, and this permitted the existence of a multiplicity of religious groups. The First Amendment clause "Congress shall make no law respecting an establishment of religion, or prohibiting the free exercise thereof" firmly established the concepts of national religious freedom and separation of church and state. Mead stresses that these provisions "were conceived in actual religious pluralism and dedicated to the proposition that all religions are equal." [17] As the nation's history unfolded in the nineteenth century, it appeared that Protestant Christianity was the national religion. However, the coming of large numbers of immigrants who were Roman Catholic and Jewish in their religious convictions challenged the Protestant consensus, and the full protection of the Constitutional guarantee of religious freedom was extended to cover them as well.

There were some restrictions in that certain religious practices (such as polygamy) were forbidden. The principle, as established in a 1944 Supreme Court decision (*United States v. Ballard*), was that, while freedom to act is limited, freedom of belief is absolute. Thus, the state would never be permitted to interfere in questions of religious doctrine and faith. Recent decisions have affirmed that religious practices may be abridged only when it has been shown that a compelling state interest outweighs the person's interest in religious freedom. Moreover, the courts have even begun to explore the possibility of broadening the definition of religion. One widely used definition, "Belief in a relation to a Supreme Being involving duties superior to those arising from any human relation" (Universal Military Training and Serv-

[17] *Ibid.*, p. 199.

ice Act of 1948), excludes from the protection of the
First Amendment the exercise of secular conscience. In
another section of the law, personal religion (the solitary
man who is not associated with any church) is also
excluded as a valid form of religious expression for purposes of conscientious objection to military service.[18]
The fact that such problems would ever arise indicates
the increasingly pluralistic nature of American society. It
is well to remember that, in order to guarantee religious
freedom to some, the framers of the Bill of Rights included the clause guaranteeing it to all. Whether they
ever conceived the matter would go this far is impossible
to determine, but it is certainly the logical fulfillment of
American pluralism.

One would never get the impression from the current
behavior of the United States that it is a "Christian
nation." American culture is, in the words of Harold
O. J. Brown, "a pornographic and nihilistic swamp that
would have made a decadent Roman blush." [19] Honesty
is hardly a characteristic of public administration from
the highest national to the lowest local levels. American
foreign policies are based on a strange mixture of self-interest, opportunism, ruthlessness, and humanistic idealism. The disease of racial prejudice has infected the
entire society. Only a minority of Americans are active
attenders and supporters of local churches. Are these the
hallmarks of a distinctively Christian nation, or are they
simply the characteristics manifested by humans? Pete
Young recently pointed to a glaring flaw in the Christian
America hypothesis which every evangelical should notice. In his inaugural prayer on January 20, 1969, Billy

[18] These matters are discussed in Milton R. Konvitz, *Religious Liberty
and Conscience: A Constitutional Inquiry* (New York: Viking, 1969).
[19] Brown, *op. cit.*, p. 72.

Graham acknowledged "Thy divine help in the selection of our leadership each four years." Commenting on this, Young raised some searching questions. Would Graham contend that divine help was manifest in Dallas on November 22, 1963? And if not on that occasion, then why on any other? Does God really have anything at all to do with the slush funds, goon squads, ghost writers, security men, and the bribes and intimidations of a national election in this country? "Surely, it is doing God no favor at all to imply that He has somehow put His *imprimatur* on our electoral process, even when that process is operating normally." [20]

Evangelicals make a great mistake when they say that America is a Christian nation. In spite of James Murch's contention that evangelicals look upon the United States "as a Covenant nation" and because of this they "believe that the highest role our nation can play is to reflect His righteous will in national and international affairs," [21] this teaching is a modern heresy and should be avoided. Foy Valentine correctly observed that "no nation with a human government can ever be a Christian nation." It may approximate Christian ideals, but nevertheless it is secular by definition.[22]

Some evangelicals try to build a case for a Christian state by appealing to the Old Testament account of Israel as the covenant people of God, but this argument is defective for two reasons. First, in Hosea 11:1 the point is made that a people becomes God's people be-

[20] Pete Young, "Trading Absolution for Support," *Christianity and Crisis*, Vol. XXIX (June 9, 1969), p. 163.

[21] Murch, "A Covenant Nation," *United Evangelical Action*, Vol. XVI (July 1, 1957), p. 7.

[22] Valentine, *Citizenship for Christians* (Nashville, Tenn.: Broadman: 1965), p. 31.

cause he calls them; they do not just simply decide to serve him. Second, God has a new covenant people, the Christian church, the body of all believers located in every land. Israel had been a small in-group, but God enlarged this to embrace the entire human race. The church is the only genuine Christian "nation," and it transcends national, racial, geographic, and cultural barriers. Christ is the supreme head of this commonwealth, and all who give themselves over to him receive citizenship in it. In other words, the universal body of believers corresponds today in the divine program to ancient Israel. There is no biblical basis for a Christian nation that corresponds to a secular state.

The American Civil Religion

If America is not a Christian nation, how does one explain the existence of so much religious symbolism in her culture, the use of God's name in the national motto, anthem, and pledge of allegiance, the practice by political leaders of publicly seeking divine assistance and invoking God's blessings, and now even the holding of religious services in the White House? The answer lies in an examination of what Robert N. Bellah designates the "American civil religion." He argues that there are certain common elements of religious orientation which the great majority of Americans share. These played a crucial role in the development of this country's institutions and continue to provide a religious dimension for the whole fabric of American life, especially the political sphere. The public religious dimension is expressed through a set of beliefs, symbols, and rituals in which all Americans share or are expected to share. The civil religion is not the antithesis of Christianity, but yet it is neither sectarian in itself nor in any specific sense Christian. It is not seen as a substitute for Christianity, as the doctrine of religious liberty leaves a wide sphere of personal piety and voluntary social action to the religious institutions. The churches are not to exercise control over the state nor is the state permitted to control the churches. Thus, the civil religion is not worship of the nation but an understanding of the American experience in the light of ultimate and universal reality.[23]

There are a number of elements in the civil religion. The inauguration of the President reaffirms the religious legitimation of the highest political authority. The idea is expressed that the rights of man do not come from the generosity of the state but rather from the hand of God. The rights of man are more basic than any political structure, and the state structure may be altered if it fails to fulfill this primary function. Thus, the revolutionary significance of America is reasserted as references are made to God's blessing and providence in the inaugural addresses and prayers. The notion is that America is worthy of God's benevolence and is carrying out the divine mission in the world for which she was chosen.[24]

Of course, the God of the civil religion is a rather unitarian and austere deity. He is related more to order, law, and right than to salvation and love. This fact is exemplified by the terminology used when his name is mentioned or his favor invoked. Such expressions as the "Invisible Hand," "Almighty Being who rules the universe," "Great Author of every public and private good,"

[23] Robert N. Bellah, "Civil Religion in America," in Donald R. Cutler, ed., *The Religious Situation 1968* (Boston: Beacon, 1968), pp. 334–35, 341, 354.
[24] *Ibid.*, pp. 335–36.

"benign Parent of the Human Race," "Providence,"
"Patron of Order," "Fountain of Justice," "Protector in
all ages of the world of virtuous liberty," "that Infinite
Power which rules the destinies of the universe," "that
Almighty Being whose power regulates the destiny of
nations," and other similar names for the biblical God
are found in the inaugural addresses of American Presidents. Although every expression characterizes God in
some way, not one of them mentions Jesus Christ, and it
is thus possible to conclude that the American civil
religion is not itself Christianity.[25] In fact, one of the
great prophets of the civil religion, Josiah Strong, wrote
that "the teaching of the three great fundamental doctrines which are common to all monotheistic religions is
essential to the perpetuity of free institutions, while the
inculcation of sectarian dogmas is not. These three doctrines are that of the existence of God, the immortality
of man, and man's accountability. These doctrines are
held in common by all Protestants, Catholics, and
Jews." [26] The civil religion is so broadly defined that
almost all Americans would have no difficulty in accom-
modating to it.

The God of the public religion is actively involved in
history and has a special concern for America, which is
his Israel, his covenant people. Europe is Egypt and
America the Promised Land. He led his people to the
New World in order to establish a new kind of social
order that would be a light to all nations. The American
Revolution was the final act of the Exodus from the old
lands across the seas. The Declaration of Independence
and the Constitution were the sacred writings of the

[25] *Ibid.*, p. 339.
[26] Quoted in Mead, *op. cit.*, p. 201.

American Israel, and George Washington was the Moses
who led his people out of tyranny into freedom. Like the
Jewish Passover, the Thanksgiving Day ritual integrated
the family into the civil religion.[27]

The Civil War added the theme of death, sacrifice,
and rebirth to the official religion. This is symbolized in
the life and death of Abraham Lincoln and the sacrifices
of the soldiers who gave their lives in the conflict. Lincoln was the "martyred President," and the war dead
were those who "gave the last full measure of devotion"
so that the country could be saved and Americans could
live in freedom. Arlington National Cemetery soon became the most hallowed monument of the civil religion
as a portion of the dead of each succeeding war was
interred in its confines. The Tomb of the Unknown
Soldier is located here, and more recently it has become
the final resting place of another martyred President,
John F. Kennedy, and his brother Robert who also fell in
the service of his country. The observance of Memorial
Day gives ritual expression to the themes of death and
sacrifice, and integrates the local community into the
cult. The whole community rededicates itself to the
martyred dead, the spirit of sacrifice, and the American
vision.[28]

It is significant that the relations between the civil
religion and the Christian churches in America have
been quite harmonious. The American civil religion has
never been anticlerical or militantly secular, but rather it
borrowed so selectively from the Christian religious tradition that few people saw any conflict between the two.
As Bellah shows, the civil religion may be utilized in a

[27] Bellah, *op. cit.*, pp. 340–42, 345.
[28] *Ibid.*, pp. 343–45.

positive manner, such as the reenactment of the sacrifice
theme in connection with the assassination of President
Kennedy or to mobilize public support for a strong vot-
ing-rights bill as President Johnson did in 1965. But the
civil religion may be invoked in favor of evil causes as,
for example, the chauvinistic God-and-country talk of
the Far Right, which aims at squelching dissent and
criticism of current American policies. The theme of the
American Israel was used to justify the shameless geno-
cide practiced against the Indians, and the sacrifice
theme is now being used to justify present American
foreign policies, above all, the involvement in Southeast
Asia.[29]

The popular image of Christian America has little to
do with faith in Jesus Christ; rather, it is a manifestation
of civil religion. Jesus gave his life for individuals, and
conversion is an individual matter, not a national one.
The dream of "national repentance" so often expressed
by pastors and evangelists across this land is only that—a
dream. The realization of a truly Christian nation lies
yet in the future, after the coming of Christ and the
establishment of his perfect rule on earth. Harold
Brown's suggestion that America is a pagan nation inhabited by a minority of committed Christians is the
reality of today.

The Dangers of Christian Americanism

There are several reasons why the concerned evangelical should have nothing to do with the doctrine of Christian Americanism. First, it has been cultivated and ex-

[29] *Ibid.*, pp. 348–50.

ploited by the Far Right, and because of this, genuine patriotism has been weakened and American democracy has been distorted. Speaking at Carl McIntire's Bible Believers' and Patriot's March in Trenton, New Jersey, Governor Lester Maddox of Georgia declared:

> If we could have our whole nation marching for victory over Communism and victory of Americanism, victory for God and victory for our children . . . then the enemies of all that is good and decent in America would surely tremble in their boots. . . . Only by raising the banner of Christ and the flag of true Americanism over every home, every business and every public building can we keep others from unfurling their banners bearing a red star, a black panther or some other foreign emblem over our nation's capital.[30]

Those who are familiar with Maddox' views know that he means that freedom of dissent must be suppressed in the name of Americanism, and he is invoking the name of Christ to reinforce his position.

In *The New York Times* it was recently noted that a growing number of people are avoiding the American flag because they feel it has become a symbol of the Far Right. To them displaying the flag is a manifestation of opposition to social progress by minority groups and all-out support for the Vietnam War.[31] This points up the fact that the superpatriots are undermining the position of millions of Americans who love their country but would not unreservedly commit themselves to a "my country, right or wrong" stance. The marriage of evangelical Christianity, political conservatism, and Christian

[30] *Christian Beacon*, Vol. XXXIV (October 30, 1969), pp. 1, 7.
[31] *The New York Times*, July 4, 1969, p. 23.

Americanism leaves the moderates no place to go. It is becoming practically impossible for them to express meaningful religious convictions and patriotic feelings under such conditions.

Further, the Radical Rightists have enlisted many conservative Christians in their struggle against American democracy. Verne Kaub asserted that "democracy is government by men, not a government of law, and to its chief promoters, democracy is synonymous with socialism." He added that majority rule is heresy to all Christians and that "the teaching profession should abstain from its ceaseless prattle about democracy" because the Communists have "adopted" the word and are using it for the party's own purposes.[32] Carl McIntire put it a little differently: "Satan has been very successful in getting us to discontinue the use of the word 'republic.'"[33] Christian leaders such as these are subverting American democratic institutions and upholding the political and economic goals of the rich who desire to maintain the *status quo*. The truly patriotic American evangelical will have nothing to do with this kind of doctrine.

A second danger of Christian Americanism is that it blurs the line of separation between church and state. The involvement of the churches in the promotion of the civil religion distracts them from performing their primary task of preaching the Gospel and meeting human needs. The possibility that the churches could be taken over by the state and transformed into mouthpieces for official policy always lurks in the background. There is some indication of movement in this direction now. Reinhold Niebuhr suggests in *Christianity and Cri-*

[32] Kaub, *Communist-Socialist Propaganda in American Schools* (Pittsburgh: Laymen's Commission of the ACCC, 1967), pp. 78, 84.
[33] McIntire, *"Author of Liberty,"* p. 169.

sis that President Nixon's practice of holding religious
services in the White House is producing a quiet, unoffi-
cial establishment of religion which "throws the aura of
sanctity on contemporary public policy." The sermon of
a Jewish rabbi at one of the White House services gives
some indication of the conforming nature of the "tamed
religion" expressed there:

> I hope it is not presumptuous for me, in the presence of
> the President of the United States, to pray that future his-
> torians, looking back on our generation, may say that in a
> period of great trial and tribulations, the finger of God
> pointed to Richard Milhous Nixon, giving him the vision
> and wisdom to save the world and civilization, and open-
> ing the way for our country to realize the good that the
> century offered mankind.[34]

The excesses of Christian Americanism are also undermining confidence in the public schools. The Supreme
Court decisions in 1962 and 1963 which prohibited the
use of prescribed prayers and devotional Bible readings
in the public schools elicited a storm of protest that has
not yet completely died out.[35] In the Regents' Prayer
case (*Engle* v. *Vitale*) the court held that a school could
not compel a child to pray, nor could it word a prayer for
him to use. (It also did not prevent a child from praying
on his own if he wished.) In the Bible reading cases
(*School District of Abington Township, Pennsylvania,*
v. *Schempp* and *Murray* v. *Curlett*) the court ruled

[34] Reinhold Niebuhr, "The King's Chapel and the King's Court,"
Christianity and Crisis, Vol. XXIX (August 4, 1969), pp. 211–12.

[35] The question of religion in the public schools is treated in easily
understandable terms and from an evangelical standpoint in two works,
James V. Panoch and David L. Barr, *Religion Goes to School* (New
York: Harper & Row, 1968), chaps. 1–3; and Donald E. Pitzer, "Christianity in the Public Schools," in *Protest and Politics*, pp. 150–181.

against required prayer (prescribed use of the Lord's Prayer) and devotional Bible reading.

In the 1963 cases the high tribunal stressed that it had no intention of eliminating all use of the Bible. It was worthy of study for its literary and historic qualities, and a study of the Bible or of religion, when presented objectively as part of a secular program of education, was quite acceptable. Justice Tom C. Clark, the writer of the decision, later insisted that "the public school may sponsor the *study*, but not the *practice* of religion." [36] The latter is the function solely of the churches in the pluralistic society of modern-day America. Unfortunately, some timid school administrators misunderstood the decisions and overreacted by trying to eliminate all traces of religion from their institutions. *Christianity Today* reported the case of a high school principal in California who tried to prevent one of his students from witnessing to his Christian faith on campus, but the boy's right to free speech was upheld by the local judicial body. [37] In short, the actions of the Supreme Court aimed at preserving the religious freedom of all Americans by prohibiting the state from coercing the practice (or nonpractice) of religion by individual persons.

Evangelicals should welcome this affirmation that the state has no business engaging in the propagation of religion, and in fact they should have challenged the practice of state-sponsored devotional exercises long before the matter came to court. Donald Pitzer correctly observes: "Any religious exercises devised by the state to satisfy virtually everyone cannot be considered true reli-

[36] Interview with James V. Panoch, recounted by Panoch in an address at the annual meeting of the Evangelical Theological Society in Cincinnati, December 30, 1969.

[37] Richard Taylor, "God Goes to High School," *Christianity Today*, Vol. XIV (December 5, 1969), pp. 48–49.

gion. . . . Such insipid ritualism cannot be tolerated as a substitute for the vital conversion experience and committed Christian life." [38] Many did approve of the action, including the editors of *Christianity Today,* but many others lashed out against it, saying that the Supreme Court decisions had "taken God out of our schools." Of course, the absurdity that human beings could take God out of anything—or could put him back in something—was never comprehended by these folks.

One reaction to the "secularization" of the schools was to press for a Constitutional amendment to set aside the court decisions by permitting prayer and Bible reading in the schools, but neither the Becker nor the Dirksen Amendment has so far succeeded in winning Congressional approval. Another response has been the creation of Christian Day Schools by evangelicals not associated with denominations that have traditionally supported school systems on theological grounds (such as the Seventh Day Adventists, the Christian Reformed, and the Lutheran Church-Missouri Synod). This new development is particularly significant because of the rapidly growing number of Protestant parochial schools and the rationale behind some of them. Many large churches now possess the facilities to house a Christian Day School, and the ideological pressures are certainly there. An article in *United Evangelical Action* pointed out that an important factor behind the interest in opening Christian schools "is the growing feeling that public schools are failing to teach patriotism and respect for America's proud heritage." [39] An editorial in the same publication declared: "If the public schools become sub-

[38] Pitzer, *op. cit.,* p. 178.

[39] William C. Moore, "What's Behind the Growing Interest in the Christian School Movement?" *United Evangelical Action,* Vol. XXIV (June, 1965), p. 10.

versive of Christian truth, we are under divine compulsion to provide separate Christian schools for our children and youth." [40] James DeForest Murch insisted that
Christian Day Schools "can make a tremendous contribution in building again the foundations which have
undergirded American institutions and inculcating those
moral and religious principles which have made America
great." [41]

The apprehension that the schools are no longer
teaching the values of the civil religion is what lies behind these statements. The hang-up on Christian Americanism obscures the fact that the schools in an increasingly pluralistic society cannot teach the practice of
religion, and incessant attacks on the secularism of the
public school can only weaken their effectiveness in
carrying out their task of educating America's youth. But
this fact leaves the schools vulnerable to the machina-
tions of Far Rightists who desire to gain control of the
schools and convert them into agencies of political indoctrination.

A fourth danger of Christian Americanism is its inability to evaluate critically the achievements and failings
of the United States. George L. Ford suggests that the
communists have induced Americans "to carry self-criti-
cism too far," while Benjamin Weiss contends: "The
United States of America has reached a high pinnacle of
advancement among the nations of the world. . . . History records no other national progress of such dimen-
sions and with such acceleration. Our nation has become
the outstanding validation of the soundness of Western
Christian culture and civilization." [42] Too many Ameri-

---

[40] "God Save Our Schools!" *United Evangelical Action,* Vol. XVI
(September 1, 1957), p. 7.
[41] Murch, *Teach or Perish,* p. 109.
[42] Ford, *op. cit.,* p. 36; Weiss, *op. cit.,* p. 9.

can Christians, filled with patriotism and love for their country, are unwilling to take a long, hard look at the country's foreign and domestic policies and say, "We have failed to measure up to our national purpose." They quote Proverbs 14:34: "Righteousness exalts a nation, but sin is a reproach to any people." But they define national sin only in individualistic terms—adultery, narcotics, murder, theft—and denounce individual criminals. Yet, they fail to see that prejudice, poverty, injustice, immoral business practices, and warmongering are the truly national sins. Those who speak out against these evils are all too frequently labeled as subversive and un-American, when in reality they are the prophetic voices in the land.

The most serious failing of all is, however, the idolatrous relationship of Christianity with American nationalism. This is a type of idolatry for the simple reason that it equates the American system with God's will and in effect demands a final allegiance and prior loyalty which belongs to God. The deity and religion are used to serve national interests and national purposes. James E. Wood places his finger directly on an open sore when he declares that in America "Christianity is readily embraced by nationalism and indeed is blatantly identified with Americanism and the American way of life." [43] David Moberg does the diagnosing: "There is no perfect institution on earth. . . . For this reason no earthly political organization should be equated with perfect or ideal Christianity. To do so would be to sanctify that which is unholy. It would amount to a form of idolatry." [44]

[43] James E. Wood, Jr., "The Problem of Nationalism in Church-State Relationships," *A Journal of Church and State,* Vol. X (Spring, 1968), p. 261.
[44] Moberg, *op. cit.,* p. 96.

The tragedy of linking Christianity to American nationalism is that it negates the role of the faith in society. Christianity becomes merely a religion that induces self-righteousness and promotes self-interest—in short, a culture religion, not a vibrant, living faith. Evangelicals need to understand that "to be a good American and to be a good Christian are not one and the same and can never be." [45] All human institutions, including the organized church, the state, the international community of nations, stand equally and directly under the judgment of God. There are no exceptions. The individual Christian's primary loyalty is to God, not the state or nation. He is first a Christian and then an American, or member of some other nationality. A marriage between Christianity and Americanism is an Unequal Yoke because one clearly stands in a superior relationship to the other. The biblical teaching is clear and unequivocal. "You shall have no other gods before me" (Exodus 20:3). "Seek ye first the kingdom of God, and his righteousness" (Matthew 6:33 KJV). Christian Americanism . . . must it be? The answer that comes from God's word is a firm and resounding *no!*

[45] Wood, *op. cit.*, p. 263.

V The Big Stick or the Old Rugged Cross

If your enemy is hungry, give him bread to eat; and if he is thirsty, give him water to drink. (Proverbs 25:21)

Then Jesus said to him, "Put your sword back into its place; for all who take the sword will perish by the sword." (Matthew 26:52)

To counteract Communism, we need *courageous action*. Firmness is the only thing which Communists understand. Firmness must be backed up by military strength and force. . . . We should remind the Communists of their treaties and our rights, and declare that we will maintain access to Berlin whatever comes, even if this means using atomic weapons. (Harold John Ockenga, address at the 1961 N.A.E. Convention) [1]

A contemporary approach to beating swords into plow-shares would be to turn the forces of technology to the alleviation of the poverty, suffering, and ignorance that have plagued mankind. Negatively, it would involve a cre-

[1] Ockenga, "The Communist Issue Today," *Christianity Today*, Vol. V (May 22, 1961), p. 12.

ative effort to prevent the use of those forces to destroy, depersonalize, or manipulate mankind. (Ross Coggins) [2]

The Development of American Militarism

One of the most unpleasant things about present-day America is that she has become a militaristic nation.[3] The country possesses a military establishment of staggering proportions which is fueled by a huge defense industry and backed by millions of proud, patriotic, and often bellicose citizens. Foreign observers have long noticed the growing power of the war lords, and some suggest that "the United States is as much in the grip of the military as were the Germans and Japanese before World War II."[4] The military is ready with contingency plans involving large joint Army–Air Force–Navy–Marine task forces which can move at a moment's notice to defend American interests and safeguard allies whenever and wherever communist aggression is suspected. The awesome size and power of the military establishment prompted President Eisenhower in his farewell address on January 17, 1961, to warn the nation that:

[2] Coggins, *To Change the World*, p. 23.

[3] Christians in the historic peace churches (Mennonites, Friends, and Brethren) have long spoken out against militarism, but other evangelical voices have been for the most part strangely silent. One striking exception to this is the hard-hitting work by American Baptist Culbert G. Rutenber, *The Dagger and the Cross: An Examination of Christian Pacifism* (Nyack, N.Y.: Fellowship, 1958). Two especially noteworthy contributions by Southern Baptist spokesmen are the symposium edited by Foy Valentine, *Peace! Peace!* (Waco, Texas: Word, 1967), and the article by William W. Cuthbertson, "The Christian, the American Military Establishment, and War," *Protest and Politics*, pp. 66–93.

[4] Murray D. Lincoln, President of Nationwide Insurance Co., writing in his firm's house organ and quoted in Fred J. Cook, *The Warfare State* (New York: Collier Books, 1964), p. 273.

This conjunction of an immense military establishment and a huge arms industry is new in the American experience. The total influence—economic, political, even spiritual—is felt in every city, every state house, every office of the Federal Government. . . .

In the councils of Government, we must guard against the acquisition of unwarranted influence, whether sought or unsought, by the military-industrial complex. The potential for the disastrous rise of misplaced power exists and will persist.

We must never let the weight of this combination endanger our liberties or democratic processes. We should take nothing for granted. Only an alert and knowledgeable citizenry can compel the proper meshing of the huge industrial and military machinery of defense with our peaceful methods and goals, so that security and liberty may prosper together.[5]

How large has the military-industrial complex become? In a syndicated article which appeared in newspapers across the nation in October, 1967, Fred S. Hoffman reported that "the mightiest concentration of economic power in the world today is the U.S. Defense Department." It annually spends more money than the combined budgets of several medium-sized countries and more than the net annual income of every corporation in America, and the prosperity, if not the actual survival, of hundreds of industries hinges upon Pentagon contracts. It had 470 major installations and over 6,000 lesser facilities and its land holdings, 27.6 million acres, are larger in area than the state of Tennessee. About 5,300 cities and towns have Defense Department projects of some kind, and Pentagon decisions transform whole communities by bringing population explosions to some and economic

[5] *The New York Times,* January 18, 1961, p. 22.

disaster to others. Approximately one out of every ten
employed Americans owes his job to defense spending,
while around 22,000 prime contractors and 100,000 sub-
contractors are enjoying defense business. A total of 76
industries is classified as "defense-oriented," and the
huge aircraft and shipbuilding industries derive over one
half of their income from military expenditures. A Congressman who fails to secure defense contracts for his
district or loses a major installation is in grave danger of
defeat in the next election, whereas those who are successful in this quite often become entrenched in office.
Congressmen who generally support economy in government will fight vigorously those budget cuts that affect a
military installation or a defense contract that means
prosperity for their constituents. Accordingly, they are
vulnerable to political pressure from the administration
concerning other legislation.[6]

The development of American militarism has been
the phenomenon of the last three decades. Before World
War II Americans were for the most part isolationist,
pacifist, and neutral if not downright hostile to the military. The regular peacetime military establishment was
quite small and had only limited influence on national
affairs. The total size of the Army and Navy in 1940 was
not much over 400,000. World War II changed all of
this, as 15 million Americans donned the uniforms of
the country's armed forces. At the same time the great
business corporations were brought into the defense effort, and they were awarded the lion's share of the war
contracts. The scale of the war and the world power
relations which resulted from it created the American
military giant. In the postwar years, especially after the

[6] *Terre Haute* (Ind.) *Tribune-Star*, October 15, 1967, p. 29.

emergence of the Cold War, military leaders came to play a major role in the formation of national policies, while retired officers occupied more and more positions of prominence in government and business.

Moreover, America is now a nation of veterans. Millions were indoctrinated in the military way of life, until by 1968 the total number of living veterans had reached over 23 million, or about 20 percent of the adult population.[7] This means that most middle-aged business, government, civic, and professional leaders have given a portion of time to serving their country in uniform. As one leading military figure points out:

> Their military training and experience have affected them, for the creeds and attitudes of the armed forces are powerful medicine, and can become habit-forming. The military codes include all the virtues and beliefs used to motivate men to high principle: patriotism, duty and service to country, honor among fellowmen, courage in the face of danger, loyalty to organization and leaders, self-sacrifice for comrades, leadership, discipline, and physical fitness. For many veterans the military's efforts to train and indoctrinate them may well be the most impressive and influential experience they have ever had—especially so for the young and less educated.[8]

As the veterans grow older, they tend to romanticize and exaggerate their own military experiences, and a great many become pugnacious and chauvinistic in their outlook. They easily fall in line with groups that favor military solutions to world problems and often assert that the younger generation needs to experience the military service and sacrifice they did.

[7] Gen. David M. Shoup, "The New American Militarism," *Atlantic Monthly*, Vol. CCXXIII (April, 1969), p. 52.
[8] *Ibid.*

The defense-related industries form a powerful lobby and are intimately linked with the military. Former officers fill many of the executive posts in defense-related industries, while the various military service associations provide opportunities to make contacts with industry and propaganda for the viewpoints of the respective services. The military-industrial complex has in turn sought to instill military values in the public. For thirty years Americans have been fed a steady diet of war toys and games, war stories (movies, novels, comic strips, television shows), and news about battles and military operations. So, for many persons military training and combat actions are merely the natural continuation of the entertainment and games of childhood.

The hard-core professional military leaders are, in the opinion of retired Marine Commandant General David Shoup, the root of America's evolving militarism.[9] They comprise a carefully trained and tightly organized group of top-caliber men who have survived perhaps the most rigorous selection system in any profession in order to reach the upper echelons. They have demonstrated their competence as planners, organizers, and leaders, and they are characterized by deep loyalty to their service and a single-minded determination to see that their point of view wins out. Moreover, because of the keen competition, a shooting war is a vital necessity for getting ahead. In combat one can best display the heroic and distinguished qualities that gain the attention of superiors and result in advancement. The rivalries among the various services are particularly severe, and each wishes to be the first to fight in any situation. Thus, readiness and speed of deployment become ends in

[9] *Ibid.*, p. 53.

themselves, and American interventions are characterized by massive and rapid action, as in the near-invasion of Cuba in 1962, the storming of the Dominican Republic in 1965, and the rapid buildup in Vietnam after the Gulf of Tonkin incident.[10]

Another feature of American militarism is the overweening role which military leaders play in dictating national policy, a phenomenon particularly evident in the 1960's. In spite of loud protests from the Far Right about the "no-win" policy in Vietnam, most competent observers of the conflict concede that the military commanders have largely managed the war and that they were the ones most willing to see the United States more involved in combat. Certainly much of the responsibility for having misrepresented the actual political situation there rests upon the military leaders, especially the ones who promoted the simplistic idea that communism can only be stopped by armed power. But the defense establishment has a willing body of supporters among the American people to whom they can appeal. The slogans of patriotism, national defense, and anticommunism have worked effectively to get military appropriations from Congress and to win enthusiastic support from the public, a large portion of whom are themselves veterans of military service and who are willing to stand behind their country, right or wrong.

The frightening implications of an unrestrained military establishment are intensified by the nuclear arms race. All the old concepts of armed strength, victory, and survival have been rendered obsolete, and no longer can nations hope to enhance their power by adding to their arsenals, recruiting larger armies, or increasing industrial

[10] *Ibid.*, pp. 53–55.

production. In the event of a full-scale war, all would be destroyed in thirty minutes. Even though the military establishment is aware that it has enough nuclear weapons to destroy the Soviet Union many times over, it still continues to demand more and more money for weaponry research. This takes place in spite of the fact that throughout the twenty-five-year history of the arms race, the United States has always led and the Russians have followed. This was true with the atomic and hydrogen bombs, long-range bombers, and nuclear missiles, and one fears that this will be the case with the Anti-Ballistic Missile (ABM) and the Multiple Independent Reentry Vehicle (MIRV) systems as well.

In 1969 the Pentagon played on American fears to squeeze appropriations for the creation of an ABM system, but at long last Congress did not roll over and play dead before the hitherto omnipotent military-industrial complex. Substantial data had by this time become available to show the utter folly of permitting nuclear explosions to take place in the atmosphere. Ernest Sternglass' research on the effect of strontium 90 on children showed the real possibility that the explosion of enough ABM warheads to fend off a Russian first strike would produce a sufficient amount of radioactive poison to insure that few, if any, children in the world would survive to maturity, and thus the human race would perish from the earth.[11] The ABM controversy, along with the Vietnam fiasco, offers some hope that in the 1970's the military will have to behave more circumspectly than they have in the past.

According to the latest reports the United States has

[11] Ernest J. Sternglass, "The Death of All Children: A Footnote to the ABM Controversy," *Esquire*, Vol. LXXII (September, 1969), pp. 1a–1d.

about 40,000 nuclear bombs and missiles, with about 2,000 maintained in an on-target position and 2,000 more in nuclear submarines roaming the oceans. In one storage depot near Albuquerque, New Mexico, there are enough nuclear weapons to destroy all life on earth. The weapons on hand in the Earle Naval Ammunition Depot in New Jersey could wipe out New York City should an accident occur, and the terrifying thing is that accidents do happen. One needs only to reflect on the number of crashes of B-52 bombers which were carrying nuclear weapons. For example, one went down near Goldsboro, North Carolina, while carrying a 25-megaton bomb, and the recovery team found that five of the six safety locks to prevent its explosion were in a "go" position.[12] What if the one remaining lock had gone? Would the Pentagon button-pushers have realized what happened, or would they have interpreted it as a Russian attack and advised the President to unleash the entire American nuclear arsenal?

If this were not shocking enough, the United States and other powers now possess enough quantities of chemical and biological warfare agents to destroy all mankind many times over. Congressman Richard McCarthy in his chilling report on CB warfare aptly names germ war as "truly the deadly fourth horseman of the Apocalypse."[13] In spite of the recent revelations about accidents involving nerve gas and biological agents and the public outcry over the use of "nontoxic" chemi-

[12] "Hope and Paradox in Nuclear Arms," *Between the Lines*, Vol. XXIX (February 1, 1970), p. 4.
[13] Richard D. McCarthy, *The Ultimate Folly: War by Pestilence, Asphyxiation, and Defoliation* (New York: Knopf, 1969), p. 60. Nigel Calder, ed., *Unless Peace Comes: A Scientific Forecast of New Weapons* (New York: Viking, 1968), reinforces the horrifying prospect of war in the 1970's sketched by McCarthy.

cal weapons in Vietnam (tear gas and defoliants), the
military, in its usual oblivious manner, continues the
research in and production of CB weapons.

A disturbing aspect about the development of American militarism is that many evangelical Christians have
been found among the ranks of its supporters. In a
widely acclaimed speech from the Capitol steps in
Washington on February 3, 1952, Billy Graham declared: "We must maintain strong military power for
defense at any cost." [14] James Murch wrote in his organ:
"Propaganda for peace is the opiate by which the non-
Communist world is to be made insensible to the dangers of Communism and the Moscow dictatorship." [15]
Christian Church leader M. M. Blair sold out lock,
stock, and barrel to the militarists when he insisted that
"those little watered-down, thin-blooded, spineless souls
who pride themselves in their non-resistance do not even
understand the ABC's of the program and nature of
Jesus. Jesus was not the 'Prince of Peace' at any price. He
is the 'Prince' of only a just and righteous peace." [16]

Even nuclear war is not out of the realm of possibility.
Harold Ockenga was quoted earlier as saying access to
Berlin must be maintained even if it required "using
atomic weapons." Lt. Gen. William K. Harrison went
even further to suggest that if the United States were
attacked by another nation, nuclear retaliation would be
morally justified. "The massive destruction caused by
nuclear weapons is not an ethical bar against their use in
a war justifiable by other moral considerations." [17] Dr.

[14] *Congressional Record*, 82d Cong., 2d Sess., 1952, Vol. XCVIII,
Part 9, A1160.
[15] Murch, "The Nature of the Beast," *United Evangelical Action*,
Vol. XVI (February 1, 1958), p. 7.
[16] Blair, *Christ, Communism, and Christianity*, p. 139.
[17] William K. Harrison, "A Christian General's View: Is Nuclear
War Justifiable?" *Christianity Today*, Vol. VII (June 21, 1963), p. 5.

Bob Jones, Jr., in his own inimitable style maintained that "if it is necessary to drop an atomic bomb on Hanoi in order to end the [Vietnam] war and save the lives of our American boys, we should do so. The cowardice of our statesmen, so-called, and their groveling fear of Red China is nauseating." [18] Of course, many of these statements were made some years ago, and one may hope that these evangelical leaders have moved away from such positions during the intervening time.

The Impact of Militarism on the American Way of Life

Future historians will look back on the decade of the 1960's as the most critical period in American history since the Civil War. At that time the virus of militarism which had infected the nation's spiritual veins finally produced a disease which threatened to destroy America. This malady was the Vietnam War. The tragedy was that so few Americans really understood what the war was all about or the reasons for the widespread opposition to it. To make matters worse, evangelical Christians seemed incapable of providing guidance for their country in those dark crisis hours. Support for the official policy on Vietnam echoed from pulpits across the land, and accounts of the tragic sufferings of the Vietnamese Christians issued steadily from the lips and pens of evangelical ministers and writers.[19] What understanding of

[18] Quoted in Campbell, *Spectrum of Protestant Thought,* p. 99.
[19] One of the best examples of this type of literature is James C. Hefley, *By Life or by Death* (Grand Rapids, Mich.: Zondervan, 1969). It is an account of the evangelical missionary effort in Vietnam with particular emphasis on the 1960's, and it blames the communists for all the sufferings which were inflicted upon the Vietnamese Christians,

the complex issues in Vietnam could be gained from the
assertion of a Florida Presbyterian minister that victory
would give us "only the satisfaction of knowing that a
ruthless and savage enemy has been forced to retire to its
own enclave, and a pastoral and peaceful people has
been restored to freedom"? [20] Was it all as simple as
Sherwood Wirt put it? "Vietnam becomes the same
basic issue that free men have faced in two World Wars
and Korea: *Will a man fight for his freedom? Because if
he won't, in a sinful planet he will not have it long."* [21]

The truth is that America sowed the wind of militarism for a quarter century and reaped the whirlwind of
national disaster in the form of Vietnam (Hosea 8:7).
The "new morality" of militarism fastened its grip upon
the country, beginning with the conflict itself. "Pacifica-
tion" meant forcing peasants to abandon their villages
and to be herded into camps established by the military
while American soldiers slaughtered their animals and
burned their dwellings to the ground. The "search and
destroy" operation was the killing of as many of the
enemy or suspected enemy as possible and then bulldoz-
ing their bodies into mass graves. Bombing was designed
to inflict the maximum suffering on its victims, such as
the fragmentation bombs, which would kill or mutilate
everyone within range of the flying metal, and napalm,
the gasoline jelly that would stick to and char human

---

while overlooking the provocations caused by their outspoken anti-
communism. For an evangelical discussion that gets at the basic historical issues behind the Vietnam conflict and reveals the complex
nature of the problem, see Robert G. Clouse, "The Vietnam War in
Christian Perspective," *Protest and Politics*, pp. 252–71.

[20] Carroll R. Stegall, "God and the U.S.A. in Vietnam," *Eternity*,
Vol. XIX (March, 1968), p. 41.

[21] Wirt, *Social Conscience of the Evangelical*, p. 125. (Italics in
the original.)

flesh. The enemy were not even human beings, but rather "gooks." The GI's in Vietnam, their moral sensitivities completely paralyzed by the bitter conflict, were able to commit cold-blooded murder as evidenced by the My Lai massacre which came to light in November, 1969. Robert Linder rightly asked: "Is the United States losing its soul in Vietnam? Can minds harrowed by brutality and accustomed to violence as a way of life ever really be normal again?" [22]

This is directly related to the erosion of traditional American values which was taking place at the same time. Lying by military officials became the order of the day, whether it was the cover-up of the accidental nerve-gas poisoning of sheep at the Utah CB Warfare testing area in March, 1968, the falsified "body counts" in Vietnam, or the cost overruns of new instruments of warfare. With these examples before them, is it any wonder that government officials and business leaders saw nothing particularly reprehensible in taking liberties with the truth in their deeds and actions? Violence became a prominent fixture of American life, since the military had educated the people to accept violence through this war. Thus, more and more of those who wished for change in the social and political order saw direct action in the streets as the answer. The idealism of nonviolence, as symbolized by Martin Luther King, Jr., is dead—the victim of an assassin's bullet. Society has been brutalized as successive generations of young men have been trained to hate and kill. Many have exalted the right to bear arms to a higher level than such liberties as freedom of speech, worship, and trial by jury.

[22] Robert D. Linder, "Vietnam: What Is at Stake?" *Congressional Record*, 90th Cong., 1st Sess., 1967, Vol. CXIII, Part 10, 12573.

A further by-product of Vietnam has been the erosion of civil liberties. Dissenters have become increasingly unpopular in this country, as revealed by the great outpouring of support for the Chicago police and the manner in which the 1968 Democratic Convention disorders were handled. The Vietnam Moratorium activities in the fall of 1969 aroused public antipathies, even to the point that some high-school teachers in an Indiana community (including a former student of this author) were severely disciplined for participating in one of these observances. Many would gladly see open disagreement with government policy made an act of treason. Rep. Joe Pool of Texas urged that war be declared in Vietnam so that the "peaceniks" could be brought under the sedition laws and "the Justice Department could move them to concentration camps and leave them for the duration of the war." Florida Congressman James Haley displayed even less charity when it came to flag burners: "I'd take them 200 miles out on the ocean, tie an anchor around their necks, throw them overboard and let them swim to any country whose flag they can respect." [23] Where will all this lead? None other than Dr. Fred Schwarz suggests: "If breakdown of law and order becomes sufficiently widespread, it is conceivable that military leaders may consider it their patriotic duty to take control and to restore order, if not law. There may even be a large body of public opinion clamoring for them to do this." [24] Could it be that the land of the free and the home of the brave is ripe for a fascist military takeover?

Militarism is driving the country toward bankruptcy and has grossly perverted national priorities. In 1968–69 defense-related spending (Defense Department appro-

[23] Newspaper clippings quoted in Dan Wakefield, *Supernation at Peace and War* (New York: Bantam Books, 1968), pp. 7, 30.
[24] *Christian Anti-Communism Crusade Newsletter,* June 1, 1969, p. 7.

priations, the space program, veterans' benefits, and interest on the portion of the national debt incurred in connection with past military costs) totaled $106.7 billion. All federal expenditures came to $136.3 billion, thus meaning that the military outlay amounted to 78.5 percent of the federal budget. This figure is more than the entire amount of federal, state, and local expenditures on health, hospitals, education, old-age benefits, welfare, unemployment, and agriculture. Direct defense spending in the decade 1959–1968 was double the amount spent for new housing (public and private) and almost twice as much as the federal, state, and local governments provided for education.[25]

To put this in perspective, the authors of the report of the Congressional Conference on the Military Budget and National Priorities pointed out:

> This order of priorities prevails at a time when twenty million Americans live in dilapidated, rat-infested housing while the building industry cannot even keep up with the population increase and is in fact declining in productivity; when there are at least ten million victims of malnutrition and untold thousands of children with permanent brain damage because of insufficient food; when close to forty million people live in poverty with little access to medical or welfare care; when millions of children are doomed to lives of misery and poverty because of inadequate or nonexistent school facilities.[26]

Economist Kenneth Boulding's remark about the imbalance in national priorities ought to be taken to heart by every Christian. He notes that the American eagle is

[25] Data taken from the report of the Congressional Conference on the Military Budget and National Priorities, March 28 and 29, 1969; published as Erwin Knoll and Judith Nies McFadden, eds., *American Militarism 1970* (New York: Viking, 1969), pp. 4–5, 86.
[26] *Ibid.*, p. 5.

portrayed in the national emblem as holding an olive
branch in one claw and a bundle of arrows in the other,
and then asks: "What kind of policy is it that weighs
down one claw with eighty billion dollars worth of arrows and provides the other with a minute, wilted olive
branch costing practically nothing?" [27]

Vietnam put such an intolerable strain on the American economy that the passing of the 1960's saw a level of
inflation approaching runaway proportions, while at the
same time interest rates were soaring and the stock market was declining. Many people were asking if the bub-
ble being blown by the military-industrial complex was
about to burst? In short, militarism is now threatening
to destroy the American way of life. The national moral
fiber has been torn asunder, traditional freedoms are
being laid on the shelf, violence and brutality have become everyday occurrences, and the economy is teetering
on the brink of collapse. Can Christians remain silent in
the face of all this?

Biblical Teaching on War

Although there is no systematic treatment of the problem of war and peace in the Bible, there are principles
expressed that shed light on the question. Those who
feel that Christians should be actively involved in warfare usually point to the abundance of Old Testament
references to soldiers, weapons, battles, and destruction
of enemies. But as Culbert Rutenber suggests, "The wars
of the Old Testament were condoned under historic
circumstances that are obsolete, and that can never

[27] *Ibid.*, p. 91.

recur." [28] Israel was God's chosen people and the enemies they fought were God's enemies. However, as it was
mentioned in the previous chapter, the church is God's
covenant people today, and the idea of a Christian nation as such is a myth. Thus, how can one determine
who the enemies of God are in order to make war against
them? World War I saw both sides contending that they
were fighting for the cause of righteousness and were the
instruments of God, and that the other side was the enemy of God and civilization. A further question: which
leaders will receive the revelation from God as to when
to go to war and when to cease fighting? Was Lyndon
Johnson directed by God to step up the level of American
action in Vietnam in 1965? Also, may contemporary
Christians, who feel their government is fighting a just
war, support the idea of exterminating entire peoples,
such as was done to the Amalekites (I Samuel 15:2–3)?
The Christian should recognize that the Old Testament
was fulfilled in the New Testament (Matthew 5:17,
Hebrews 1:1–2, 8:13) and therefore his stand for or
against war must be based on an understanding of New
Testament principles.

Christ's statement "Render therefore to Caesar the
things that are Caesar's, and to God the things that are
God's" (Matthew 22:21) seems to separate the specifically Christian responsibilities from the duties to the
state, and it has been used to justify doing whatever the
state wishes, including killing people in the waging of
war. However, Jesus did not specify what Caesar's due is,
and he definitely did not say that Caesar and God are
equals and thus have equal rights to the Christian's

---

[28] Rutenber, *The Dagger and the Cross*, p. 77. Many of the ideas in
this section have been drawn from chapters 3, 4, and 5.

allegiance. Further, Jesus did not imply in any way that
the ruler has any rights which are independent of God
and his will. Because all belongs to God, Caesar has only
those rights which God grants to him, and they may be
revoked at any time the ruler violates the purposes of
God.

The passage in Romans 13 that requires everyone to
"be subject to the governing authorities" because they
"have been instituted by God" does not mean unques-
tioning obedience to the state. It does mean that the
principle of government is part of God's intentions for
men, and therefore the Christian must be as good a
citizen as he possibly can within the limitations of Scripture and his conscience. The principle of government is
in accordance with the will of God because it provides
order and dispenses justice. This does not mean that a
particular government is necessarily God-ordained, for in
fact a Hitler or a Stalin may be so corrupt and evil as to
create a system born of hell. The very fact that government is instituted by God means that it is limited, and
the principle expressed by Peter and the apostles, "We
must obey God rather than men" (Acts 5:29), takes
precedence over the dictates of the state. It is nothing
short of blasphemy to say that the Christian owes un-
qualified obedience to the state. Thus, a Christian cannot justify his support of the regime's military endeavors
merely by falling back on the excuse "The Government
tells me I must fight." He must have a better reason than
that.

Of course, the New Testament does not specifically
pass judgment on the military profession, but on the
other hand Christ's commendation of Zacchaeus, the
chief tax collector (Luke 19:5,9), is no indication that
he condoned graft and political corruption. Luke 3:14

clearly indicates that, whereas our Lord did not consider the soldier's profession as evil per se, he would not countenance the use of it as a cloak for willful violence, personal or national character assassination, and greedy self-interest. Jimmy R. Allen suggests that the general silence of the New Testament concerning things military occurs because the early Christians did not have to face the question of participation in warfare. Jews and slaves were exempt from service in the Roman armies, and at that time conscription was seldom necessary to meet military manpower requirements. The Roman legions were the police power of the day, making basic law and order dependent on their presence. The first Christians lived in a world where military might was a major factor in the social order, but they did not need to come to terms with the matter of a personal relationship to the problem.[29]

Culbert Rutenber points out four New Testament principles that relate to the question of war and peace.[30] First, *a bad means corrupts a good end.* The idea that it is right to do evil that good may result was rejected by Paul (Romans 3:7,8), while in his temptation at the outset of his public ministry (Matthew 4:1–11), Christ rebuffed Satan's efforts to persuade him to use the wrong means to reach the right end. If one does evil in order that good may come of it, what results is something not very good. The story of modern war is doing good— "make the world safe for democracy," "guarantee the four freedoms," "stamp out Nazi (communist, imperialist) tyranny." The ends are good but the means— namely, mass slaughter and violence—are not. When

[29] Jimmy R. Allen, "The Bible Speaks on War and Peace," in *Peace! Peace!* pp. 28–29.
[30] Rutenber, *The Dagger and the Cross,* pp. 48–70.

one gets on the end-justifies-the-means toboggan, there is
no stopping until he hits bottom. Once man resorts to
violence, it will escalate as he uses more and more terrible weapons to gain an advantage over his opponent.
"War, like God, is no respecter of persons. Its corrosive
taint falls upon the just and unjust alike."

The second principle is *by their fruit ye shall know
them.* Jesus taught that a sound tree brings forth good
fruit and a bad tree evil fruit (Matthew 7:15–20), and
the same principle is applicable to human society. What
are the fruits of war? They are the death of thousands if
not millions, intense human suffering and misery, utter
moral degradation, economic dislocation, mass destruction of property, and other similar evils. All the basest
passions in the human personality emerge in time of war
as the restraints are removed from man. War takes a
heavy toll in spiritual casualties as well, because it has
such a shattering effect on a person's Christian faith, and
many who return from the conflict are lost to the service
of Christ and the church. These are the fruits of modern
war—are its origins good or bad?

The third principle is *active, outgoing love, even to
enemies.* The emphasis on positive, selfless love is central
to Christianity. Because it is never self-centered nor does
it expect anything in return, the same principle should
determine the Christian's relationship with his adver-
saries. In the Sermon on the Mount (Matthew 5:38–47)
Christ set forth the idea that one should express divine
love by seeking the good of his enemies. Paul stressed
that the aspect of God which should be imitated and
embodied in one's actions is his mercy, not his wrath—
not vengeance or retributive justice (Romans 12:19).
Even if a war is the judgment of God on one's opponent,
nowhere in the New Testament is it intimated that

Christians should help God to carry out his chastisement.

The fourth principle is *active warfare against evil with the weapons of good will*. "Do not return evil for evil or reviling for reviling; but on the contrary bless" (I Peter 3:9). "Love your enemies and pray for those who persecute you" (Matthew 5:44). "Never avenge yourselves, but leave it to the wrath of God. . . . If your enemy is hungry, feed him; if he is thirsty, give him drink. . . . Do not be overcome by evil, but overcome evil with good" (Romans 12:19–21). The returning of good for bad is a more effective "vengeance," because the very idea of vengeance itself is transformed so as to become the victory of Christian love. "The Christian avenges himself by triumphantly loving his tormentor in spite of the latter's evil enmity." This breaks the chain reaction by which evil produces evil. By doing this, the person is following the example of Christ who triumphed, not by inflicting evil but by bearing it in his own person on the cross (I Peter 2:21). The Christian is to follow in his steps and also overcome evil with good.

Onward Christian Soldiers?

Christians through the centuries have developed elaborate cases for and against participation in their countries' wars, and the prowar group has invariably been in the majority. This is certainly true with American evangelicals, except those in the historic peace churches. They can easily be induced to support any military venture by the United States which professes to be aimed at "stopping communism." Evangelist John R. Rice said he had "no doubt that if there is ever holy and righteous cause for war, it is to prevent godless communism with its murder and torture and persecution from taking over other lands which ask our help." [31] The vice-president of the Christian Anti-Communism Crusade, Texas businessman William P. Strube, declared that we are "Christian soldiers" doing battle against communism and therefore we must put on the full armor of God (Ephesians 6:10–18). "In this armor there is one part of the anatomy that is not protected—the back. God meant for us to be 'onward' Christian soldiers and not 'backward' ones." [32]

Obviously, many evangelicals would not go as far as these spokesmen do, but they would say that there are times when a person must fight for what he believes is right. They would point out that war is sometimes the lesser of two evils; that is, there are situations in which one kind of killing is less evil than another kind. For example, it is difficult to defend a policy of not having done anything to halt the aggression of Adolf Hitler and prevent him from committing further atrocities against the Jews and the peoples of Eastern Europe. But it must never be forgotten that the sword of this argument also cuts two ways. Can the mass murders of thousands of civilians in the bombings of Hamburg and Dresden be justified? Or what about the alliance with Stalin who was equally as wicked as Hitler? The lesser-of-the-evils argument must not be invoked simplistically.

Unfortunately, it is difficult to escape the conclusion that the real reason for Christian support of wars is often not so much the question of justice or righteousness as it

[31] John R. Rice, *War in Vietnam: Should Christians Fight?* (Murfreesboro, Tenn.: Sword of the Lord, 1966), p. 18.
[32] William P. Strube, Jr., *The Star over the Kremlin* (Grand Rapids, Mich.: Baker, 1962), p. 76.

is such human considerations as pride, fear, and national self-preservation. This is definitely the case when in the United States military activity becomes related to a deeply rooted messianic consciousness. The fondly held belief that our cause is good and that of the communist countries is evil clearly reveals that Americans are just as capable of self-righteous delusions as any other people. Evangelicals need to be aware of this and avoid an automatic linking of God's purposes to American military endeavors. A statement like "If we valiantly defend our Christian civilization by every known device in peace and war, the 'second Dark Age' of world Communist rule will not come" [33] simply is not acceptable to the Christian who has any real understanding of world affairs. The thoughtful believer will also have difficulty with the related notion that America is losing out in the world because she has turned away from God, and if she does not repent of her national sin, she will suffer military defeat at the hands of her enemies. Billy Graham has been a consistent exponent of this view, as for example:

If our nation at this hour would turn to the Word of God, if the men and women who make up our nation would put their trust in Jesus Christ, then I guarantee on the authority of God's Word that the enemies at our gates could be pushed back; God would intervene and put them to flight. . . .

We have the most powerful military force the world has ever known, but we are afraid to use it. The will to fight for freedom and justice is gone. . . . I am convinced that if our leaders would lead the American people in repent-

[33] Blair, *op. cit.*, p. 137.

ance of sin and in faith in Jesus Christ, God would do the
fighting for us.[34]

Especially as a result of the Vietnam conflict, more
and more young Americans have adopted the position
that they will not fight in wars which they believe are
morally wrong. Evangelicals should welcome this display
of spiritual vigor, and in fact, some have. According to a
report in the *Christian Century,* sixteen faculty members
at Fuller Theological Seminary in March, 1968, submitted an open letter to President Johnson requesting a
change in the selective service laws to allow conscientious objection to wars which young persons believe to
be "unjust and immoral." [35] The steadily rising number
of registered conscientious objectors and the tempo of
protests against the Vietnam War which characterized
the 1960's have made it patently clear to the Pentagon
officials that in future conflicts they will not be able to
count so heavily on large numbers of "Christian soldiers" to come rushing enthusiastically to the colors.
Political considerations and military expediency alone
will not be adequate; the military leaders will have to
consider the moral implications of an undertaking before
committing the nation. The dedicated Christian will
have no difficulty in agreeing with Charles A. Wells that
this development "marks a spiritual advance of
significance." [36]

The military offers America the "big stick," while the
Christian has "the old rugged cross." The church, as the

[34] Graham, *God and the Nations* (Minneapolis: BGEA, 1964), p.
8. (An *Hour of Decision* radio sermon.)

[35] *Christian Century,* Vol. LXXXV (April 24, 1968), p. 508.

[36] "War & the Conscience of Youth," *Between the Lines,* Vol. XXIX
(January 15, 1970), p. 4.

editor of *Christianity Today* points out, has at its disposal a spiritual force which has nothing to do with violence but yet is the "ultimate weapon." [37] This spiritual power, if allowed to work, will transform the structures of life and society. Violence seldom leads to a better life because all too often the one who takes the sword ends up a victim of the sword. The evangelical Christian must say to his fellow citizens: "Lay down your foolish national pride and greed and turn to the Lord, for in him lies your confidence."

[37] "Force: A Christian Option?" *Christianity Today,* Vol. XIV (January 30, 1970), p. 20.

VI American Responsibility in a Shrinking World

But I say to you, Love your enemies and pray for those who persecute you, so that you may be sons of your Father who is in heaven; for he makes his sun rise on the evil and on the good, and sends rain on the just and the unjust. (Matthew 5:44,45)

Then the righteous will answer him, "Lord, when did we see thee hungry and feed thee, or thirsty and give thee drink? And when did we see thee a stranger and welcome thee, or naked and clothe thee? And when did we see thee sick or in prison and visit thee?" And the King will answer them, "Truly, I say to you, as you did it to one of the least of these my brethren, you did it to me." (Matthew 25:37–40)

The roots of the United Nations are in religious humanism, and the U.N. will flourish in spite of all its abject failures as long as these roots remain strong. Only a return to orthodox Christianity can shatter the messianic humanism of the United Nations. (Rousas John Rushdoony, Presbyterian minister and author) [1]

[1] Rousas John Rushdoony, "Has the U.N. Replaced Christ?" *Your Church—Their Target,* p. 233.

156

A fundamental obstacle to peace is the deprivation of mankind, both individually and corporately. There can be no peace within man, peace in his family, peace within our communities or peace in the world until we seek to fulfill the total needs of mankind. The call to evangelize is a call to proclaim and to love. It is a call to respond to the needs created by unjust social conditions and it involves us totally in peacemaking. (Sen. Mark Hatfield at the U.S. Congress on Evangelism) [2]

Blessed Are the Peacemakers

With the balance of nuclear terror in the world, American statesmen are faced with the problem of creating an international order that will enable the competing political ideologies to exist together in peace. Evangelical Christians ought to be fully behind this vital endeavor, but because of the Unequal Yoke, far too many have been dragging their feet. It does the cause of national security and international harmony no good when evangelicals decry efforts to promote peaceful coexistence through negotiations with communist states and to foster understanding among nations by active participation in international organizations such as the United Nations. An N.A.E. executive secretary's statement that communists "practice brainwashing on a global scale" (that is, whenever they talk about friendship, negotiations, and peaceful coexistence, they really are intent on world domination) is certain to destroy the confidence of many conservative Christians in the methodology of diplomacy and wise statecraft.[3]

[2] Mark O. Hatfield, "Evangelism and World Peace," *Decision*, Vol. X (November, 1969), p. 8.
[3] Ford, *op. cit.*, p. 35.

There are other examples of this type of behavior that
can be singled out. The prominent evangelical journalist
who lamented that "in international relations historic
ideals of justice are being abandoned for methods of
expediency" and "the bargaining method, the method of
compromise, is superseding the mighty power of moral
principle" has nothing to offer America's leaders but the
big stick (and the big bomb).[4] He is not cognizant of the
fact that compromise is the only alternative to armed
force when two sovereign entities are dealing with each
other. This contribution to the solution of the nation's
international problems falls in the same category as that
of another evangelical luminary who warned his col-
leagues about "the folly of those who talk co-existence,
rapprochement, and understanding with the Communist
state."[5] Carl McIntire has no place for diplomacy and
compromise. He tells Christians: "It is morally imperative that we seek to have the Communist world dis-
rupted and destroyed. . . . There are some things worse
than war; one of them is slavery, Communist concentration camps. It would be better to have no world at all
than to have a slave world."[6]

Fortunately, the prospect for the 1970's is that the
United States will continue moving farther and farther
away from this "holy war" psychology in dealing with
communist regimes. The country's leaders recognize that
moralistic and religious crusading is a serious hindrance
to the formulation of the compromises and accommoda-
tions without which nations cannot live together. John
Bennett correctly observed that "moralistic foreign pol-

[4] Murch, *Teach or Perish*, p. 39.
[5] Harold Ockenga, *Christianity Today*, Vol. V (May 22, 1961), p. 9.
[6] McIntire, *Servants of Apostasy* (Collingswood, N.J.: Christian
Beacon, 1955), pp. 210–11.

icies usually produce devils on the other side, and it is hard to negotiate with devils, though without negotiations there may be no future for them or for us." [7] A further danger of this type of policy in dealing with communism was noted by Herbert Butterfield. One can easily be seduced into thinking that the *status quo* should be maintained against revolution or social change and against the zeal of reformers. "One may even come to think it a virtue to preserve abusive and quasi-feudal systems against the archenemy, against the reforming ardor of Communism." [8] To see how true this comment is, one only needs to look over the roster of America's so-called "friends" and notice the number of fascist and military regimes which have received support from the United States.

It is imperative that Christians align themselves with those who seek after a more enlightened policy to deal with communism. A movement which has such an idealistic and political appeal to a large part of the world's population "cannot be successfully countered by a simple and absolute negation." It is a self-defeating approach, almost "like trying to restrain an ocean tide." [9] Urgently needed is some original thinking in the quest for a solution to the problem of coexistence in the 1970's. Evangelicals must play an integral part in this effort to bring peace to the world.

As a starting point in the quest for a more adequate policy, the United States needs to define what her core

[7] John Coleman Bennett, *Foreign Policy in Christian Perspective* (New York: Scribners, 1966), p. 19.

[8] Herbert Butterfield, *International Conflict in the Twentieth Century: A Christian View* (New York: Harper, 1960), p. 37.

[9] F. Ernest Johnson, *A Vital Encounter: Christianity and Communism* (Nashville, Tenn.: Abingdon, 1962), p. 159.

interests are and what the vital interests of the other great powers are as well. This involves determining the nature of the core interests of the Soviet Union in Eastern Europe, China in Asia, and the United States in the western hemisphere. A sane diplomacy would be oriented toward the avoidance of entanglements in the other great powers' spheres of interest. This was the mistake of Vietnam for the United States, while Cuba, a land located in the American sphere, turned out to be an albatross for the Russians and in fact almost brought a nuclear holocaust upon the world.

The fundamental assumptions which underlie American foreign policy also need to be reexamined, especially the ideas that the major communist states (Russia and China) pose a continuing threat of physical military aggression, that the spread of the political doctrine of communism can be restrained by military means, that revolutions everywhere are communist-inspired and constitute a threat to the United States, and that the United States must maintain a clear and significant military superiority over the Soviet Union, especially in nuclear arms. Had these faulty assumptions been reviewed and modified in the late 1950's, the United States could in all probability have avoided stumbling into the Vietnam quagmire. It would be in America's best interest to adopt coexistence as her basic policy and accept the territorial and balance-of-power *status quo* among the nuclear powers as permanent, while simultaneously working for neutralization of those parts of the world that lie outside the core interests of the great powers.[10]

At the same time, it should be recognized that funda-

[10] This is discussed in greater detail in *American Militarism 1970*, chap. 2.

mental changes have been taking place in the communist world. The myth of the monolithic communist political bloc has long since been discredited by the Sino-Soviet split, and variations of communism are springing up among the member states. The disarray in the world communist movement was revealed for all to see by the Soviet military intervention in Czechoslovakia and the criticism which it drew from communist parties all over the globe. No longer can it be said that there is a unified, global communist threat to the "free world." Nationalism is gaining the ascendancy over Marxism as the North Korean and North Vietnamese communists jealously guard their national interests against Chinese domination, while the Soviet bloc states in Eastern Europe, especially Romania and to a lesser extent Poland and Hungary, have cautiously been pursuing policies oriented toward more autonomy. Even in Czechoslovakia the Russians do not have a pliable stooge, in spite of the military occupation and extensive purges of the reformers in the party and government. And, of course, there is Tito and the independent course which communist Yugoslavia has pursued for over two decades.

Also, a gradual process of humanization is taking place in the European communist countries so that the quality of life for their citizens is inching upward. Even in the Soviet Union the grim brutalities of the Stalin era are past history. Granted, this movement toward freedom is small by Western standards, but it constitutes a step in the right direction and should be welcomed by Christians everywhere. It is particularly significant that the greatest pressures for liberalization are coming from the younger generation in the communist lands, and those resisting change are the aging party leaders. Some day the reins of power will be in the hands of today's youth.

Can grinding oppression last forever under these circumstances?

Thus, evangelicals should ignore those voices which urge no negotiation and no compromise with communist states. Even though the differences seem insurmountable now, there is no reason to assume that areas of agreement and common concern could not be spelled out. Both the United States and the Soviet Union have an interest in scaling down the superheated arms race and diverting the resources consumed here to meeting domestic problems. Both have good reasons to see an equitable and lasting settlement in the Middle East worked out. The world is simply too small to permit the animosities to continue indefinitely.

Another way to promote peaceful relations between East and West would be to increase trade. Not only could this work toward a more normal world economy, but it also could be mutually beneficial. To refuse to trade with another country merely for ideological reasons is cutting off one's nose to spite his face. Moreover, cultural exchanges should be fostered, and the number of scholars, students, and travelers going in both directions should be increased as much as possible. Well-conceived and executed exchange programs could do a great deal to bring about understanding, appreciation, and respect on the level of people-to-people relationships. Also, the United States should maintain diplomatic relations with the *de facto* regimes of all states. The policy of refusing recognition to Red China, Cuba, and some other communist governments serves only to alienate these countries and peoples and insures that they will be antagonistic toward the United States.

The Christian's attention in all of the above matters is directed toward the divine ideal for the world—peace.

Peace is a significant theme in both the Old and New Testaments and above all in the life of Christ. Lutheran Ralph Moellering reminds Christians that their concern for peace "must emphasize that nuclear war is a greater danger to freedom than Communism at its worst." The moral fiber of civilization might never survive the shock of a nuclear exchange.[11] Committed Christians must do everything possible to alleviate conditions that might lead to all-out war, because the Prince of Peace has commissioned them to do so (Matthew 5:9). It is not merely a "humanistic assumption" to say that war is the greatest of all evils, in spite of C. Gregg Singer's remark to that effect in *Christianity Today*,[12] and evangelicals would do well to heed Mark Hatfield's words in his address to the U.S. Congress on Evangelism in September, 1969: "It is hypocritical for a Christian to claim he has the peace of God in his heart if he remains oblivious to the violence and destruction in the world." [13]

The road to peace and freedom will not be an easy one to follow. Some may try to dodge the responsibility of working for peace by saying that sin makes peace impossible or that there will be no peace on earth until the Second Coming of Christ. But does the continuing existence of disease until the Parousia justify indifference toward the hostilities and sufferings of society? Charles Wellborn suggests some practical steps toward peace that American Christians should follow. First, they must divest themselves of national self-righteousness, honestly recognize their nation's internal problems, and wholeheartedly give themselves to the continuing task of find-

[11] Moellering, *Modern War and the Christian* (Minneapolis: Augsburg, 1969), p. 77.
[12] *Christianity Today*, Vol. XII (November 24, 1967), p. 31.
[13] Hatfield, *op. cit.*

ing solutions to them. Second, they must seek to find
legitimate and nondestructive avenues where international frictions, disagreements, and conflicts of interest
may be aired openly and honestly and the conflicts ad-
justed. Third, they must have patience with the slow
processes of diplomacy and negotiation and not allow
themselves to be rushed into hasty actions, especially a
military showdown. Finally, they must have confidence
in their values and way of life and also in God. "As
Christian citizens, committed irrevocably by our Gospel
to the cause of peace, we must throw our weight behind
honest, hard-headed, realistic attempts to find a path of
peace through the perilous mine field of modern international relationships." [14]

Assistance to Less Fortunate Nations

The United States is the wealthiest nation in history
and has for a number of years shared a portion of her
bounty with the less well-endowed nations in the form of
food shipments, farm machinery, technical assistance,
and military equipment, as well as cash grants and low-
interest loans. This has been endorsed by most Americans either because they were convinced that it was in
the national interest to do so or they felt some vague
sense of obligation for the poorer peoples of the world.
Political conservatives in America, however, have almost
to a man opposed foreign aid, and the evangelicals who
identified with conservatism stood solidly with them.
Billy James Hargis claimed that American foreign aid
paid "much of the cost of the subversion and capture by

[14] Charles Wellborn, "Practical Steps for Peace," in *Peace! Peace!*
pp. 154–61.

Soviet Russia of nation after nation." [15] Howard Kershner contended that it "interferes with and discourages
indigenous production and in many cases probably ends
up doing more harm than good. It teaches dependency
and discourages effort." [16] Edward Coleson called foreign
aid "a global give-away" and insisted that if the people in
the backward areas "were honest, diligent and frugal,
and if their government were stable and responsible, just
anyone with a little money and the spirit of adventure
would go there and start an industry." [17] There is perhaps
a grain of truth in some of these objections, but un-
doubtedly one of the most irrational criticisms was heard
at a small discussion group sponsored by the Christian
Anti-Communism Crusade. A person remarked that the
surplus food given by the United States to nations like
India to feed starving multitudes decreased the number
of people the "communist rulers" in these countries had
to feed themselves. They then could spend that extra
money on airplanes and weapons.[18]

The dedicated Christian finds these arguments against
foreign aid hollow, to say the least. When he sees the
human misery in the world, he realizes the need to do
more than dispense such moralisms as "they need to be
more honest and diligent." He finds it difficult to visual-
ize how the less-developed countries will ever overcome
their enormous social and economic problems without
help from the wealthier nations. Actually, the values of
Western civilization are being put to the test at this

[15] Hargis, *op. cit.*, p. 137.
[16] Kershner, "Debate on Foreign Aid," *Christian Economics,*
Vol. XXII (January 6, 1970), p. 3.
[17] Coleson, *op. cit.*, pp. 340–41.
[18] Reported in Mark Chesler and Richard Schmuck, "Participant
Observation in a Super-Patriot Discussion Group," *Journal of Social
Issues,* Vol. XIX (April, 1963), p. 27.

point. As Victor Ferkiss suggests, if we in the West are not willing to work and sacrifice to reduce human wants and to bring about conditions under which individuals can fully develop their capacities, "we are confirming the Communist lies by default." If the West is not able to mobilize itself to work effectively toward these goals, the feeling is certain to grow in the non-Western world "that we do not in fact deserve to win in the struggle with Communism." [19]

It is difficult to force American evangelicals to face up to this burning issue, largely because they cherish a number of myths about the world in general and world poverty in particular. Daniel Grant, a Southern Baptist political scientist, has identified four of these attitudes which are held by far too many Americans.[20] First, they feel that what happens to Americans is more important than what happens to foreigners. This is reflected in such things as high protective tariffs against foreign products manufactured by "cheap labor," stringent restrictions on immigration from the more populous parts of the world, and demands for sharp cuts in American aid to poor nations. This is also evident in the vast proportion of church funds which is allocated to erecting new structures and supporting cumbersome denominational bureaucracies, while only a pittance is designated for foreign missions. Second, world poverty is primarily the result of laziness. This overlooks the many other factors which produce poverty, for example, illiteracy, overpopulation, disease, war, and simply the absence of opportunities for employment which exist in technologically backward and capital-starved areas.

[19] Ferkiss, *op. cit.*, p. 156.
[20] Daniel R. Grant, *The Christian and Politics* (Nashville, Tenn.: Broadman, 1968), pp. 109–14.

Another myth is that communism is obviously worse than the existing governments in Asia, Africa, and Latin America. Because communism is tolerated and often looked up to by many people in these areas, they do not deserve American help. It would be better to shore up the governments with military assistance rather than help the people to have a better standard of living. Finally, it is argued, the world does not need American economic aid—it needs the Gospel. The Christian must not be diverted from his mission of reaching lost men with the Gospel. The time is short—men are dying and Christ's coming may be at any moment. While we are distracted by meeting the bodily needs of people, thousands if not millions will be slipping away into a Christless eternity.

It cannot be stressed too strongly that the concerned evangelical must throw off these pitiful rationalizations and begin working to alleviate suffering in other parts of the world. What should he do? First, he will seek God's guidance to determine if he ought to serve in some capacity abroad, and he will pray for and contribute to missionary agencies that endeavor to bring both the Gospel and the "cup of cold water" to needy peoples. Further, he will play his part in influencing public opinion and bringing pressure to bear on his government to fulfill its responsibilities to less fortunate peoples around the world. This would involve not only foreign aid but also the removal of trade barriers so that the underdeveloped countries can market their products. Also, the Christian will support family-planning measures that will help these people to control their burgeoning populations.

A meaningful foreign-assistance program will be costly, but the United States should not shrink from her responsibility to help the poorer nations. Americans are reputed to spend $3 billion a year on house pets, $5 billion on tobacco, $9 billion on liquor, and $30 billion on gambling,[21] so it seems that a little bit can be spared for other peoples in the world. Also, if the appalling rate of defense spending could be scaled down, there would be more money available for economic aid to developing countries. The concerned evangelical must face the reality that the deprivation of a large portion of mankind constitutes a formidable obstacle to peace today. If he is to be a peacemaker, he must seek to fulfill the total needs of man. Thus, part of the call to evangelize is bringing the message of the Gospel to bear on the needs created by social injustice.

International Cooperation

In the world of the twentieth century the need for international cooperation is steadily growing, and the United States has every reason to encourage moves in this direction. All nations have a definite interest in peace and safeguarding the security of one another. Also important is the existence of viable governments in these countries, regardless of their political orientations. A reasonable amount of stability within a nation is better than a condition of continuous anarchy. The economic well-being of every country is a vital necessity, and the stronger nations must help the weaker ones to achieve economic growth through trade and assistance. The United Nations could be utilized to channel development aid to the poorer nations, and in this way assist-

[21] Grant, *op. cit.*, p. 117.

ance programs could be conducted on a multilateral basis. Thus, they would not be such an affront to the sensibilities of the developing nations nor would they appear to be devices aimed at purchasing allegiance to a power bloc led by the United States, the Soviet Union, or some other country.

The use of the United Nations as an agency to promote international cooperation does not meet with the approval of all evangelicals, and in fact it has been the target of bitter attacks by many conservatives. The objections fall into three general categories, as a few selected examples will indicate. First, it is atheistic or humanistic. R. J. Rushdoony said the U.N. "is the new god and savior of men who have declared the God of Scripture to be dead." It is a "modern Tower of Babel" which was created by religious humanism.[22] Murch complained that the U.N.'s "moral and religious atmosphere . . . is far removed from New Testament Christianity." God was not invoked when it was formed, and "its whole structure, principle and procedure are without benefit of religion." [23] Second, it is seen as a communist plot to subvert American freedom. According to Hargis, the U.N. "is an important part of Communism's carefully conceived and brilliantly executed plan to destroy America and the free world." [24] Third, it is a world government scheme that is undermining American national independence and preparing the way for the Antichrist which is prophesied in Revelation 13.[25] As Carl McIntire put it:

[22] Rushdoony, *op. cit.*, pp. 229, 234.
[23] Murch, "Reds and the World Council of Churches," in *Your Church—Their Target*, p. 201.
[24] Hargis, *op. cit.*, p. 127.
[25] *Ibid.*, p. 134.

The United Nations is but the prelude and the instrument for bringing in one-world government . . . which, in bringing to pass its so-called economic justice and universal peace, will bring tyranny to mankind and unify world power so that one man can wield it for his own ends and to his own ends and to his own glory.[26]

It is noteworthy that those who attack the U.N. as a superstate which threatens to encroach on American sovereignty often criticize it at the very times it manifests its inability to act as a superstate—for example, during the Hungarian uprising of 1956 or the Czechoslovakian invasion in 1968. Reinforcing the idea that the U.N. offers no real threat to American national self-interest, the data compiled by the World Rule of Law Center at Duke University on the votes taken on major resolutions reveal that the United States was never on the losing side of issues which were of vital importance to its security interests. And the Soviet Union never won on a major resolution which it introduced and which the United States opposed![27] It is the Soviet Union that has constantly tried to block U.N. actions with vetoes, not the United States.

The United Nations is not a superstate or a federal union of nation-states but simply an association of states. It is not a world government although many of its founders had hoped it would evolve into one. The U.N. has made a number of contributions which should be pointed out. Through its charter it has provided an expression of moral and legal principles to which nations are committed. Although members cannot be forced to

---

[26] McIntire, *Servants of Apostasy*, p. 220.
[27] Wellborn, "The United Nations, An Instrument of Peace," in *Peace! Peace!* pp. 91–92.

obey these principles, they can be put on the defensive for violating them. The U.N. provides an opportunity for the representatives and often the leaders of nations to meet without fanfare and publicity and discuss issues, both major and minor. It is a place where diplomacy takes place continuously, even between the East and West. It is a forum where world opinion can be aired, problems clarified, and tendencies toward polarization on issues modified. The new nations and their representatives have the opportunity to gain status and international experience, because here, as equals, they can express themselves and begin learning the facts of international life.

The United Nations has many practical achievements to its credit in peacekeeping and separating combatants. Korea set an example of multilateral action in resisting aggression, one that was not possible in Vietnam, in spite of America's efforts to involve her allies in the conflict. Although the U.N. has had only limited success in the continuing Palestine crisis, it was able to bring peace to the Congo in the early 1960's and persuade India and Pakistan to cease hostilities in 1965. The specialized agencies and various allied bodies have accomplished much in such areas as food distribution, aid to children, scientific cooperation, promotion of literacy, and economic development.[28]

The ideal purpose of the United Nations was to provide an international structure that would work for the maintenance of peace. It would move in the direction of enforcing international order, yet would provide workable means for peaceful change in the relationships among nations. It is the most advanced effort so far in the

[28] Bennett, *op. cit.*, pp. 136–42.

direction of creating an international society of relative order, peace, and justice, and Christians should whole-heartedly support it. Concerning the U.N., Sherwood Wirt wisely states that "the threads of hope may be fragile but the evangelical is called to strengthen them." [29]

Even though the world is growing smaller, the prospect of a worldwide government does not lie in the immediate future. Nationalism is too strong a force to permit that to take place. What the Christian should be working for is the development of a *just* international order in which peaceful modifications of the *status quo* can take place. Further, this order should be one that "properly embraces all the competing nations, systems, creeds and ideologies." If peoples we do not like are excluded, they are given the license to behave as they wish and feel no obligation to observe the rules of international conduct.[30] This can hardly be regarded as responsible behavior on the part of Americans. Thus, evangelicals should be in the front rank of those who are seeking to establish a more equitable and inclusive international order, as this will benefit all mankind and glorify their Father in heaven to whom the world and all that is in it belong.

[29] Wirt, *op. cit.*, p. 125.
[30] Butterfield, *op. cit.*, p. 77.

VII This World Is My Home

I do not pray that thou shouldst take them out of the world, but that thou shouldst keep them from the evil one. . . . As thou didst send me into the world, so I have sent them into thy world. (John 17:15,18)

You are the salt of the earth; but if salt has lost its taste, how shall its saltness be restored? It is no longer good for anything except to be thrown out and trodden under foot by men. You are the light of the world. A city set on a hill cannot be hid. Nor do men light a lamp and put it under a bushel, but on a stand, and it gives light to all in the house. Let your light so shine before men, that they may see your good works and give glory to your Father who is in heaven. (Matthew 5:13–16)

This world is not my home, I'm just a-passing through,
My treasures are laid up somewhere beyond the blue;
The angels beckon me from heaven's open door,
And I can't feel at home in this world anymore.
(Popular Gospel song, author unknown)

The evangelical's social conscience requires that he play his part as a member of the team of humanity. If there is poverty, he should be taking a lead in seeking to eradicate it. If there is injustice, he should be an Amos, pointing it

173

out. If there is corruption, he should be helping to turn
the rascals out. If there is waste, he should be acting the
role of the good steward. It is in this role, rather than in
the stance of the pristine rugged individualist, that the
evangelical Christian can make his best contribution.
(Sherwood Eliot Wirt) [1]

Serving God in Contemporary Society

The link which many evangelicals have forged between Christianity and political conservatism is a disservice to Christ, because it prevents the Gospel from
exercising its fullest effectiveness in modern society.
The Gospel must stand in judgment over all political
and economic systems, but if the Christian becomes too
closely tied to one of these systems, he often is unable
(or unwilling) to criticize and work to correct its basic
flaws. It is difficult to avoid the conclusion that the
Unequal Yoke means that evangelicals who refuse to
work for the reformation of contemporary society believe
it is already Christian. If this is the case, then evangelicals should quit pretending that the Gospel is anything
more than a pious cloak for specific economic and political pressure groups. This, of course, completely misses
the point that Christianity is relevant to all ages and all
men, and it can unite people of differing political alle-
giances and economic theories. It can survive the rise
and fall of the various systems, something which philosophies bound to a particular order of things seldom can
do. One study noted that in modern times, Christians
have lived under absolute monarchy, limited monarchy,
democracy, and dictatorship. Although they are not all
equally favorable to Christianity, none of them can sepa-

[1] Wirt, *op. cit.*, pp. 76–77.

rate man against his will from the love of Christ. "No man and no system has final power over man." [2] It is clear, then, that the Christian cannot be brought into total bondage to any earthly order, as his first allegiance is to his heavenly Father.

Nevertheless, the question is often raised: why should the Christian get involved with the problems of contemporary society? Is not his home "up above"? Did not Jesus say that a person should not lay up his treasures on earth but rather in heaven and there his heart would be (Matthew 6:19–21)? Is it not true that Christians "are not of this world" even as Christ also is not of the world (John 17:16)? Is it not more important for the believer to concentrate wholeheartedly on winning souls and purifying his own life so that when he appears before the judgment seat of Christ, the Master will say, "Well done, good and faithful servant" (II Corinthians 5:10; Matthew 25:23)?

These arguments and others like them are thrown at evangelicals who try to make their brethren aware of their Christian responsibilities. But British evangelical J. N. D. Anderson, in his helpful book *Into the World*, suggests that the Christian ideal of holiness is "the life-and-death involvement of the soldier, whose mission it is to liberate enemy-occupied territory and restore it to the sway of its proper King." He sets forth some broad principles that make such an attitude of involvement imperative for the Christian. First, God created man in his own image and after his likeness (Genesis 1:26–27) and this gave man his original worth. When man fell into sin, Christ died for him, thus indicating the value which man still had in God's eyes. In the incarnation

[2] *A Christian's Handbook on Communism* (New York: National Council of Churches, 1962), p. 74.

God himself became truly man and experienced all that is humanity—joy, sorrow, hunger, thirst, weariness and refreshment, temptation, suffering, and death itself. Also, God made the material world and has a purpose for it as such. "Everything created by God is good," and should be accepted with gratitude, even where it is ministered through unbelievers (I Timothy 4:4). One can give glory to God by using created things rightly, that is, in accordance with the Creator's revealed will. Moreover, in the new creation all things will be summed up in Christ as head (Ephesians 1:10), for his cross has reconciled not only the world of men but also the whole material and spiritual universe (Colossians 1:20).

Anderson further reminds Christians that this present world is still under God's government and is very much the object of his love and concern. Christ taught that every man is our neighbor whom we must love and serve, the prophets passionately proclaimed God's demand for social justice, and the apostles stated unequivocally that human institutions such as the family and the state are ordained by God and designed to fulfill particular functions and purposes for the welfare of man. In addition, Christ emphasized to his servants that they were to be the "light" and "salt" of society, and he prayed not that they should be taken out of the world but kept from evil in it. Thus, the Christian must affirm in no uncertain terms that this is God's world, not Satan's, even though it may presently "lie under enemy occupation." God is the Sovereign Lord of the universe and not just the personal solace of individuals.[3]

[3] J. N. D. Anderson, *Into the World: The Need and Limits of Christian Involvement* (London: Falcon Books, 1968), pp. 14–15, 17. An excellent discussion of the biblical basis for Christian social responsibility may also be found in Moberg, *op. cit.*, chap. 2.

How do Christians become involved in confronting and solving problems in the world? They must be like leaven in a lump (Luke 13:20–21); that is, Christians must permeate society, ministering to their fellowmen and laboring unceasingly to make the world a better place for all people. God summons them to serve him in all walks of life to fulfill his purpose in the world. Some are called to the ordained ministry, while others to work in factories, run office machines, teach children, fly airplanes, and to thousands of other vocations. They are "his workmanship, created in Christ Jesus for good works" (Ephesians 2:10).

One of the most effective ways a Christian can assist his neighbor is through joint action of the total community, that is, governmental action. An experienced inner-city pastor in Newark, New Jersey, Howard Hageman, served notice to evangelicals that they are going to have to involve themselves more "in political struggles with the establishment" if they hope to minister to people in the ghetto. They must attack the "root causes" of substandard housing, poverty, hunger, and bad education, and "more often than not, they are deeply entrenched in the way things operate, in all kinds of traditional privilege and power. Though we cannot legislate love, we should do what we can to legislate decency and justice." [4] Although it is frequently denied that morals can be legislated, the truth is that laws can force changes in behavior patterns which in turn ultimately transform the moral climate of the community. A good example of this point is the changes that are taking place in race relations because of civil-rights legislation.

[4] Howard Hageman, "Cancelled Flight," *HIS*, Vol. XXX (December, 1969), p. 3.

How can Christians exert political influence? First, they should seek to gain accurate knowledge of current problems and needs. They should gather information from a wide range of sources representing various points of view so that when they vote, they will be able to cast their ballots intelligently.[5] Of course, every Christian ought to exercise his most fundamental civic right, the franchise. It is inexcusable that evangelicals, of all people, should fail to perform this duty. Further, they should actively participate in political organizations and parties, even though this involves cooperation with many people who are not Christians. This does not mean that the individual believer need conform blindly to the spirit and practices of the political group or abandon his moral and spiritual principles. Like all social institutions, the political party is comprised of fallen human beings and is therefore imperfect, but Christians are not for this reason exonerated from responsibility in relation to it.

Some will even be called to serve in public office, and in this way they can be especially effective in ministering to the needs of their neighbors and bringing the influence of the Gospel to bear on the vital problems of the nation. At present, a number of evangelicals occupy elective offices in Congress and state and local governments, while many others hold appointive and civil-service positions at all levels of government. Their Christian testimonies are being felt across the land as they serve as leaven on the political scene.[6] In short, every Christian

[5] See Walfred H. Peterson, "The Responsibility of the Christian Voter" in *Protest and Politics*, pp. 22–36; and Valentine, *Citizenship for Christians.*

[6] Two outstanding legislators who exemplify the type of leadership which evangelical Christians can provide are Sen. Mark O. Hatfield of Oregon and Rep. John B. Anderson of Illinois. Hatfield's views are ably set forth in his book *Not Quite So Simple* (New York: Harper &

should seek to determine what civic responsibility God has for him. Carl F. H. Henry emphasizes:

> There is no justification for a Christian to shirk his political duty and to shrink from direct political involvement. Christianity is a minority movement in an evil world gripped by complex and powerful mechanisms of iniquity, but this fact in no way excuses believers from obedience to the Lord in political affairs.[7]

Evangelicals should stand up for the weak, the poor, and exploited in today's society, because that is what Jesus did in his day. For too long justice has been denied them, and their interests have not been adequately represented in the councils of government. One of the most vital tasks for Christians is to bring about the incorporation of justice into the legislative, administrative, and judicial institutions of the federal, state, and local governments. The evangelical community can no longer sit on the sidelines of the current struggle for social justice, and serve as the passive mouthpiece of the vested interests of power and wealth who wish to maintain the *status quo*.

On the other hand, the church should not allow itself to be merely the voice for revolutionary groups which are promoting their own selfish ends. Charles Wellborn's pithy observation "Life in the Christian middle is never

---

Row, 1969) and article "How Can a Christian Be in Politics?" in *Protest and Politics*, pp. 6–21. Anderson's work in Congress is described in Wesley Pippert, "John B. Anderson: Agent of Reconciliation," *Christian Life*, Vol. XXXI (October, 1969), pp. 32–33, 72–74. See also John B. Anderson, ed., *Congress and Conscience* (Philadelphia: J. B. Lippincott, 1970).

[7] Henry, *Aspects of Christian Social Ethics* (Grand Rapids, Mich.: Eerdmans, 1964), p. 130.

easy" is certainly correct.[8] Those evangelicals who seek to
rectify the imbalance resulting from the Unequal Yoke
will be condemned by the Christian Rightists as modern-
ists, liberals, heretics, and communists. Those on the
other extreme will continue to reproach the evangelicals
for not going far enough and for their emphasis on
personal salvation.

There is also the problem of training Christians to
serve God in contemporary society. This was elaborated
by Horace L. Fenton, Jr., in his study paper at the
Wheaton Congress on the Church's Worldwide Mission
in April, 1966. He stressed that "most new Christians
need clear teaching by the Holy Spirit, through the
church, of the far-reaching implications of their new-
found faith. It is all too possible for an individual believer to fail to see the connection between his love for
God and his responsibility to his fellowmen, unless it is
pointed out to him—not just once, but many times." [9]
This message needs to be driven home to the evangelical
church in America. An extensive program of education is
urgently needed to awaken conservative Christians to
their failure to stand for justice and righteousness in
society. Time is running out for the church. Will evangelicals respond to the challenge?

Shall the Church Speak on Social Issues?

Unfortunately, evangelicals who are genuinely concerned about social involvement are deeply divided over

---

[8] Wellborn, "The Imperative of Peace in a Nuclear Age," in
Peace! Peace! p. 75.

[9] Harold Lindsell, ed., *The Church's Worldwide Mission* (Waco,
Texas: Word, 1966), pp. 197–98.

the question whether the institutional church or individual Christians should speak out on social issues. The individualist position holds that the church's function is to preach the life-changing Gospel and nurture the Christian believers. The new man in Christ will, in turn, go out into the world and work to improve the conditions of human existence. The church, as a church, is a spiritual body and is not competent to make pronouncements on political and economic questions, except perhaps to enunciate a few general principles. The concrete political-economic task is the duty of the individual Christian, and if he has submitted to the lordship of Christ, he will be zealous in the effort to bring Christian ethical principles to bear on specific political, economic, and social matters.

The individualist stance has been above all a consistent editorial policy of *Christianity Today*. Some quotations from the journal illustrate this:

> How is the voice of the Church heard? . . . Every Christian as a believer-priest has the obligation to make himself heard. Let him do so, enlightened by biblical teaching, armed with the facts, humble in attitude, and courageous in conviction. The man of faith who by word and deed discharges his Christian responsibilities in all realms of life will be used by Jesus Christ as he speaks his word of love and judgment to the world.[10]

> Although the Church has no mandate, authority, or competence to say *yes* or *no* to political and economic specifics—except perhaps in some emergency that may require a *no* to preserve the Christian faith, witness, and life—it must set the principles of revealed morality in dia-

[10] "Who Speaks for the Church?" *Christianity Today*, Vol. XI (June 9, 1967), p. 27.

logic relation to the modern alternatives. Only in this way can Christians comprehend what really governs a good political community and what really constitutes a good society.[11]

Also, the editorial evaluating the U.S. Congress on Evangelism took pains to emphasize that the call for social involvement issued there "was put on a personal basis" and that a major error of the ecumenical movement is "making the institutional church the agent of social revolution." [12] This thinking, in a somewhat muted form, also underlies Sherwood Wirt's *The Social Conscience of the Evangelical,* and it can be seen in the sermons and writings of Billy Graham.

The individualistic view of the church has always been a target for attacks from liberal circles, especially the *Christian Century,* but some of the most trenchant criticisms are to be found in the pages of an avowedly evangelical periodical, the *Reformed Journal.* For example, Lewis Smedes has raised serious doubts about the assumption that a person who is converted to Christ automatically possesses the supernatural potential to heal society's multifarious wounds. His view is that since men have rights emanating from the social spheres to which they belong, law and government can do more to combat evil and guarantee social and economic justice than the efforts of a few regenerated persons.[13]

[11] "An Ecumenical Bombshell," *Christianity Today,* Vol. XI (September 15, 1967), p. 28.
[12] "U.S. Congress on Evanglism: A Turning Point?" *Christianity Today,* Vol. XIV (October 10, 1969), p. 32.
[13] Lewis B. Smedes, "The Evangelicals and the Social Question," *Reformed Journal,* Vol. XVI (February, 1966), pp. 9–13; Carl F. H. Henry, "What Social Structures?" *ibid.* (May–June, 1966), pp. 6–7; Smedes, "Where Do We Differ?" *ibid.,* 8–10.

James Daane and Richard Mouw focus on the church's right and responsibility to take positions on specific issues. Daane points out that if the church can speak only when it has the consensus of its members, it would be deprived of any prophetic function whatsoever. The church is to speak in the name of the Lord, and even though it might err from time to time in pronouncements, this is no excuse for it to remain silent. Further, no individual Christian, speaking and acting as a Christian, can do so alone. He always speaks and acts as a corporate member of the Body of Christ, and the same holds true for the church. Then, too, by what right do many evangelical leaders, who themselves deny the right of the church to take stands on social and political issues, publicly speak out on what they consider to be the social conscience of other evangelicals? [14]

Mouw views as a sweeping denial of the church's authority the idea that the church is only to lay down a few general principles while the laity speaks on the specifics. If, on the other hand, the church is authorized to say *no* in some emergency situations, this means that not speaking is either a tacit approval of a given issue or an expression that the issue is not serious enough to consider. Thus, the church's silence becomes a kind of pronouncement. In point of fact, the presence of sin in the world provides the church with a continuing "emergency situation." Sin has permeated the hearts of men and radically affects their lives and their economic and social structures, and the church is obliged to bring to all sinful situations both the judgment and Gospel of God. [15]

[14] James Daane, "Who Speaks for the Church?" *Reformed Journal*, Vol. XVIII (May–June, 1968), pp. 17–19.
[15] Richard Mouw, "The Church and Social Specifics," *Reformed Journal*, Vol. XIX (July–August, 1969), pp. 3–4.

These criticisms are of considerable significance, because if orthodox Christianity is ever going to cut loose
from political conservatism, it will have to recognize the
fallacies of the individualistic social ethic. The evangelical church will have to assume a prophetic role and point
an accusing finger at the glaring injustices in contemporary society. It must take the lead in sensitizing the
Christian social consciences of its members and motivat-
ing them to go forth with a Gospel of compassion that
will not just prepare people for the afterlife but also
meet their present needs as well. After all, this world is
their home, and ours, too. This will be an agonizing
experience for evangelical Christianity, and it will un-
doubtedly offend many wealthy and powerful church
members who desire to preserve the *status quo*. Yet, the
church has no choice but to speak out against the ills of
the society that threaten the destruction of both church
and society.

A Glimmer of Hope

Will evangelical Christianity break loose from the
Unequal Yoke? Will the church come out and separate
itself from those selfish interest groups that throttle its
Christian witness? Many have come to regard this as
only a fond wish, but the course which the United States
Congress on Evangelism took made it patently clear that
a definite transformation in evangelical attitudes toward
social issues is taking place. Approximately five thousand
influential clergy and lay churchmen from ninety-five
denominations assembled in Minneapolis on September
8–13, 1969, with the intention of confronting current
problems in evangelism; they heard speaker after speaker

stress the need for more evangelical social concern. Such prominent personages as Oswald C. J. Hoffmann, Leighton Ford, Mark Hatfield, and Tom Skinner summoned their fellow Christians to compassionate involvement in the problems of the contemporary world. The editor of *Christianity Today* pointed out the real significance of this congress when he stated: "Perhaps no evangelical conclave in this century has responded more positively to the call for Christians to help right wrongs in the social order." [16]

An issue of *Christianity Today* which appeared some weeks after the Minneapolis gathering unwittingly but accurately revealed the current tension in evangelical circles over social involvement. In his regular column, Executive Editor L. Nelson Bell used the text "It is not right that we should give up preaching the word of God to serve tables" (Acts 6:2) to urge that evangelicals devote their wholehearted efforts to preaching the Gospel. Bell suggested that nothing could be "more disastrous for the Church and its witness in the world than for it to give the impression that it is primarily concerned with the needs of the body—economic, political, and social." He argued that inherent in the acceptance of Christ were "built-in social advantages," that is, "avenues of blessing reserved for believers alone." Christians should not commit themselves to every program of social action because some of them "are capable of doing great harm, for they would substitute revolution for regeneration, socialism for free enterprise, and in effect, Communism for Christianity." [17]

While this old warrior of the faith desperately sought

[16] "U.S. Congress on Evangelism: A Turning Point?"
[17] L. Nelson Bell, "Beware!" *Christianity Today*, Vol. XIV (October 24, 1969), pp. 24–25.

to hold back the tidal wave of change, readers of the magazine were also presented with the text of the forthright appeal for evangelical social concern which one of Billy Graham's top associates, Leighton Ford, had delivered at the U.S. Congress on Evangelism.[18] In ringing terms the youthful Ford proclaimed: "It is to the shame of the Christian Church that we have been so slow to face the demands of the Gospel in the racial revolution of our time. With some notable exceptions, we have moved only when we have been run over from behind." Further, he declared: "We need a holy discontent with the status quo. The Gospel calls for constant change. Conversion is a change of direction . . . God is not tied to seventeenth-century English, eighteenth-century hymns, nineteenth-century architecture, and twentieth-century clichés."

He courageously warned that "we should repudiate the efforts to couple evangelism with a crude, sword-rattling anti-Communism," and pointed out that "history's greatest revolution began not under a red star in Petrograd in 1917 but under the star of Bethlehem two thousand years ago." God began the great reversal in Jesus Christ, who turned human categories upside down, while the early Christians were revolutionaries in every sense of the word. "Here was a *revolutionary God*, releasing *revolutionary power* through a *revolutionary community*, in *revolutionary action*." Christian conversion was so revolutionary because it meant a complete transformation. Man's broken relationships with God, himself, and his fellowmen were healed.

Ford also stressed that a doctrine which redeemed

[18] Leighton Ford, "Evangelism in a Day of Revolution," *ibid.*, pp. 6–12.

sinning men without transforming them "into crusaders against social sin" was unthinkable. He urged Christians to be "wary of saying that the preaching of the Gospel will solve all of society's ills." For one thing, there is no biblical warrant for believing this, and besides there are "Bible belts" where, in spite of the preaching of the Gospel and the conversion of people, "the built-in structures and attitudes of prejudice" change very slowly. He insisted that Christians must be concerned "both for love and for justice." Although only the saving power of Christ can produce real love, "love is not a substitute for justice, and since not all men are or will be converted to Christ, and since even we Christians have imperfect love, we have a responsibility to seek justice in society." He noted that "a Christian politician who seeks to pass laws that create guidelines for justice is doing God's work just as truly as a Christian pastor who seeks to win the lost to Christ."

Because of the Unequal Yoke many twentieth-century evangelicals have fallen short of Christ's mark by doing little to modify the structures that have caused societal ills. However, there is hope for evangelicalism if Ford's affirmation of social concern is embraced. The road of full obedience to the commandments of Christ will not be an easy one to follow. To combat social problems will involve considerable sacrifices in time, money, prestige, and power, but Christians must be prepared to pay the costs and shoulder the burdens of loving their neighbors. The choice is ours; shall we be yoked to the world or to Christ?

Suggestions for Further Reading

The following books are recommended for those who wish to delve deeper into these matters. The basic considerations in their selection have been relevancy to the evangelical Christian viewpoint (however, not all of them are by evangelicals), willingness to confront issues in an open-minded manner, and ease of reading. Church libraries would be well-advised to purchase all of these books, and many Christians will want to obtain them for their personal libraries.

Anderson, J. N. D., *Into the World: The Need and Limits of Christian Involvement*. London: Falcon Books, 1968. A distinguished British evangelical discusses why and how Christians should become involved in the life of the contemporary world.

Anderson John B., ed., *Congress and Conscience*. Philadelphia and New York: J. B. Lippincott Company, 1970. Essays by Rep. Jim Wright, Sen. George S. McGovern, Sen. Barry M. Goldwater, Rep. Charles E. Bennett, Rep. Albert H. Quie, Rep. John B. Anderson. Six members of Congress who are practicing Christians offer a unique perspective on the problems of reconciling ethical ideals with the rough-and-tumble politics of the nation's capital.

Bennett, John Coleman, *Foreign Policy in Christian Perspective*. New York: Scribners, 1966. Shows the relevance of Christian ethics to foreign policy and urges Christians to work for a policy that is as humane and just as possible.

Butterfield, Herbert, *International Conflict in the Twentieth Century: A Christian View*. New York: Harper & Brothers, 1960. An English historian reveals the historical processes underlying the East-West impasse and points out the role Christianity can play in an age of global revolution.

Clouse, Robert G., Linder, Robert D., and Pierard, Richard V., eds., *Protest and Politics: Christianity and Contemporary Affairs*. Greenwood, S.C.: Attic Press, 1968. A collection of eleven essays on current affairs by Christian scholars which aims at disproving the stereotype that evangelicals are automatically political conservatives.

De Koster, Lester, *Communism and the Christian Faith*. Grand Rapids, Mich.: Eerdmans, 1962. The best book on communism written from an evangelical standpoint. Endeavors to show what communists really believe and how this is related to basic Christian beliefs.

Elbrecht, P. G., *The Christian Encounters Politics and Government*. St. Louis, Mo.: Concordia, 1965. A clear presentation of the American political system by an experienced politician and officeholder which argues that Christians should serve in public positions.

Grant, Daniel R., *The Christian and Politics*. Nashville, Tenn.: Broadman, 1968. Defines political problems and issues in such a way that the Christian can feel prepared to vote intelligently and urges him to become involved in practical politics.

Hatfield, Mark O., *Not Quite So Simple*. New York: Harper & Row, 1968. The political autobiography of an outspoken evangelical Christian statesman, in which he discusses his career in public life and sets forth his reasons for opposing the Vietnam War.

Henry, Carl F. H., *Aspects of Christian Social Ethics*. Grand Rapids, Mich.: Eerdmans, 1964. Discusses some of the contemporary issues in social ethics and provides some evangelical guidelines in strategic areas of Christian concern with emphasis on individualistic social action.

Jorstad, Erling, *The Politics of Doomsday: Fundamentalists of the Far Right*. Nashville, Tenn.: Abingdon, 1970. A study of the history, theology, political ideology, and action programs of fundamentalist groups which identify with the political Far Right, with particular stress upon Carl McIntire, Billy James Hargis, and Edgar Bundy.

Maston, T. B., *The Christian, the Church, and Contemporary Problems*. Waco, Texas: Word, 1968. Establishes a biblical basis for social concern and treats family, social, and political problems from this perspective.

Moberg, David O., *Inasmuch: Christian Responsibility in 20th Century America*. Grand Rapids, Mich.: Eerdmans, 1965. A timely, provocative, and uncompromising discussion of Christian social responsibility. One of the most significant books on social issues from an evangelical.

Moellering, Ralph L., *Modern War and the Christian*. Minneapolis: Augsburg, 1969. Aims at sensitizing the Christian conscience to the evils of modern warfare. An alarming and frank treatment of the problem.

Overstreet, Harry and Bonaro, *The Strange Tactics of Extremism*. New York: Norton, 1964. A careful discussion of both right- and left-wing extremism which includes some useful suggestions on how to deal with these problems.

Redekop, John H., *The American Far Right: A Case Study of Billy James Hargis and Christian Crusade*. Grand Rapids, Mich.: Eerdmans, 1968. A reasoned and dispassionate analysis of Hargis and his movement which provides valuable insight into the workings of the religious Far Right.

Rutenber, Culbert G., *The Dagger and the Cross: An Examination of Christian Pacifism.* Nyack, N.Y.: Fellowship, 1958. A careful exposition of Christian pacifism and its biblical foundations, which will challenge the reader to rethink his position on war.

Swomley, John R., Jr., *The Military Establishment.* Boston: Beacon Press, 1964. Demonstrates in a frightening manner the vast power which the Pentagon has gained and its ability to dominate American political, economic, and educational life.

Valentine, Foy, *The Cross in the Marketplace.* Waco, Texas: Word, 1966. A forthright summons to Christians to bring their faith to bear on all aspects of life.

Valentine, Foy, ed., *Peace! Peace!* Waco, Texas: Word, 1967. A symposium which attempts to deal honestly and realistically with the concept of political peace and to provide a Christian perspective on the problem.

Wirt, Sherwood Eliot, *The Social Conscience of the Evangelical.* New York: Harper & Row, 1968. A prominent evangelical journalist gives a lucid presentation of the biblical basis for social concern and challenges his fellow believers to come to grips with the pressing issues of the day.